T0366957

The POWER of SELF-CONFIDENCE

The POWER of SELF-CONFIDENCE

BECOME UNSTOPPABLE, IRRESISTIBLE, AND UNAFRAID IN EVERY AREA OF YOUR LIFE

BRIAN TRACY

WILEY

JOHN WILEY & SONS, INC.

Cover design: Paul McCarthy

Published by John Wiley & Sons, Inc., Hoboken, New Jersey.
Published simultaneously in Canada.

For general information on our other products and services or for technical support, please contact
our Customer Care Department within the United States at (800) 762-2974, outside the United
States at (317) 572-3993 or fax (317) 572-4002.

Wiley publishes in a variety of print and electronic formats and by print-on-demand. Some material
included with standard print versions of this book may not be included in e-books or in print-on-
demand. If this book refers to media such as a CD or DVD that is not included in the version you
purchased, you may download this material at http://booksupport.wiley.com. For more information
about Wiley products, visit www.wiley.com.

ISBN 978-1-118-43591-5 (cloth); ISBN 978-1-118-46400-7 (ebk); ISBN 978-1-118-46401-4 (ebk);
ISBN 978-1-118-46402-1 (ebk)

Printed and bound by CPI Group (UK) Ltd, Croydon, CR0 4YY

C9781118435915_170324

The manufacturer's authorized representative according to the EU General Product
Safety Regulation is Wiley-VCH GmbH, Boschstr. 12, 69469 Weinheim, Germany, e-
mail: Product_Safety@wiley.com.

This book is fondly dedicated to my son, David Tracy,
one of the most positive, outgoing,
optimistic, and self-confident
people I have ever met.

CONTENTS

INTRODUCTION

Entering the No Fear Zone

Nothing splendid has ever been achieved excepted by those who dared believe that something inside of them was superior to circumstance.

—Bruce Barton

Welcome to the no fear zone. In the pages ahead, you will learn how to develop confidence, courage, and unshakable determination in every area of your life. You will learn to approach the biggest challenges and opportunities of your life completely unafraid, convinced of your ability to accomplish anything you put your mind to.

The good news is that you have extraordinary potential for success, achievement, and prosperity, with more talent and natural ability than you could use in a *hundred* lifetimes. The only thing standing between you and the incredible life that is possible for you is *fear*—of all kinds—and by the time you finish this book, your fears will be gone forever.

For more than 25 years, I've studied successful men and women, looking for the characteristics and qualities they have in common that have enabled them to achieve so much more than the average person. I've read thousands of books, articles, and research studies on success, and I've come to the conclusion that the foundation quality of success in every walk of life is self-confidence.

Every man or woman who has ever accomplished anything out of the ordinary has turned out to have greater self-confidence than the ordinary person. When you develop yourself to the point where your belief in yourself is so strong that you know that you can accomplish almost anything you really want, your future will be unlimited.

The Great Question

A woman who had listened to one of my programs wrote to me recently and told me that one line in that program had changed her whole outlook on life. It was simply a question: "What one great thing would you dare to dream, if you knew you could not fail?"

When she began asking herself that question, over and over, her entire view of what was truly possible for her expanded dramatically. She saw clearly what she really wanted to be, have, and do, and she simultaneously realized that it was only fear, and doubt in her own abilities that was holding her back.

What would *you* do differently if you were absolutely guaranteed of success in any undertaking? What if some great force could endow you with the power to achieve any goal that you could set for yourself? To put it another way, what if you were completely unafraid of anyone or anything and you felt completely free to act, in any area, in your own best interests? The fact is that, if you developed the quality of unshakable self-confidence, your whole world would be different.

Unlimited Self-Confidence

With greater confidence in yourself and your abilities, you would set bigger goals, make bigger plans, and commit yourself to achieving objectives that today you only dream about. You would take whatever steps were necessary to earn more money and enjoy a higher standard of living. You would set your sights on a bigger house, a better car, more beautiful clothes, and nicer vacations. You would want all kinds of things for your family and for those close to you. You would do what you really want to do and you'd refuse to conform to the wishes or opinions of anyone else. You would define your life in your own terms and live every day consistent with exactly what it is you want, and not the wishes of other people.

With greater self-confidence, you would be a different person in every part of your work life and career. You might decide to ask for a promotion, or a raise, or even change to another job or another company, or even another industry. You would move immediately to do whatever it took to get onto the fast-track in your career.

If you are in sales, you would call on more people, make better and more forceful presentations, ask for more orders, and close more business. If you are in management, you would organize and reorganize your human and material resources to create a work environment that suited you perfectly, rather than making endless compromises in an attempt to please a variety of different people.

With greater self-confidence, you would be bolder and more imaginative. You would be more creative and willing to experiment with new and different ideas and ways of doing things. You would be willing to consider unusual and risky alternatives and be willing to commit yourself wholeheartedly to projects that are today sitting only on the back burner of your mind.

More Powerful, Popular, and Persuasive

If you had unlimited self-confidence, you would be more powerful, popular, and persuasive with other people. You would be more cheerful, likable, and welcome wherever you went. You would speak up and speak out clearly in your interactions with others, and you would be admired, respected, and sought after by everyone who knew you. Recognition and responsibilities would flow to you because of people's belief in your ability to do whatever it took to get the job done. Positions of prestige and status would open up for you and people would bring you opportunities and possibilities that you cannot now imagine.

Dealing with Difficulties

With greater self-confidence, you could deal more effectively with the inevitable problems and difficulties that arise in day-to-day life. You would think continually in terms of solutions, and how you could turn any situation to your best advantage. You would laugh at adversities that would dishearten most people and pluck success out of the jaws of failure. You would turn lemons into lemonade. You would feel invincible and unconquerable.

With higher levels of self-confidence, you would be far more effective in dealing with difficult people and situations. You would be a far better negotiator and be able to ask for, and get, better prices, terms, and conditions in everything you bought and sold.

Feel Terrific about Yourself

With greater self-confidence, with an unshakable belief in yourself, nothing would be impossible for you. More than anything else, you would feel terrific about yourself. You would feel truly happy about every part of your life, knowing deep down inside that you have the ability to take whatever steps and make whatever changes are necessary to assure that your life is exactly the way you want it.

You would experience a tremendous *sense of control*, which is the fundamental requirement for happiness, well-being, and maximum performance. You would feel like "the master of your fate and the captain of your soul."

With unlimited self-confidence, you would feel completely self-determined and in charge of your life. You would experience a feeling of strength and power and purpose, and you would have a positive mental attitude toward yourself, everyone in your life, and everything you do. With unshakable self-confidence, you would unquestionably be an exceptional human being.

You Can Develop Self-Confidence

Unfortunately, however, this is not all that easy. Most people have limited self-confidence and many people have no self-confidence at all.

Human beings tend to be plagued with doubt about their own abilities and fears about every imaginable thing, especially the unknown. The psychologist Abraham Maslow said the story of the human race is the story of men and women "selling themselves short."

The great majority of people tend to compare themselves unfavorably with others. They dwell on their own weaknesses and limitations, and they eventually settle for far less than what they are really capable of. Instead of enjoying high levels of self-esteem, self-respect, and personal pride, the average person just gets by from day to day.

If self-confidence, and the self-esteem that goes with it, is so desirable, why is it that so few people have enough self-confidence to live the lives that are possible for them? There are a thousand reasons, but perhaps the most wonderful discovery about self-confidence is that it is a mental quality that can be learned with practice. Because it is learnable, self-confidence can be developed and built up systematically and progressively over time by following the instructions in this book.

The good news is that everyone has a certain amount of self-confidence, more in some areas and less in others, and by working from that base, it is possible for you to build yourself up to the point at which you are completely confident in any area that is important to you.

The Great Law

Perhaps the most important of all the laws that govern our lives was put forth by Aristotle in about 350 B.C. He called it the "Principle of Causality," and proclaimed for the first time that we live in a universe governed by order, and that there is a reason for everything that happens.

We call it the law of cause and effect, and it is often referred to as the "iron law" of human destiny. The law of cause and effect can imprison us in a cell of our own making, or it can liberate us by giving us complete freedom, depending on how we use it. The law itself, like the law of gravity, is neutral.

This law of cause and effect, which is both a physical and a mental law, says that for every effect in our lives, there is a specific cause, or causes. If there is an effect in our life that we want more of, like more money or greater success, we can trace it back to the cause, and by repeating the cause, we can enjoy more of the effects. If we are in sales or business and we have successes, we can trace those successes back to the specific things that we did to achieve them; by repeating those causes, we can enjoy the same effects.

This law also says that if there is an effect in our lives that we don't want, whether it be overweight, insufficient funds, problems with people, or negative business conditions, we can trace that effect back to the causes, and by removing or changing the causes, we can achieve different effects or results.

This law of cause and effect is so simple and obvious that no one seriously questions it. We live in a world, and in a universe, governed by law, not by chance. Everything happens for a reason. Neither success nor failure is an accident. They have specific causes, and when we repeat the causes, we get the same effects, no matter who we are. This is just the way the world works.

The Roots of Low Self-Confidence

The world is full of people who are not happy with their results, and yet they continue to do the same things, think the same thoughts, say the same things, and take the same actions, every day, and they are amazed that they continue to get the same negative effects. Einstein's definition of insanity was, "continuing to do the same things and expecting to get different results." However, this is simply not possible.

The law of cause and effect applies with equal validity to our levels of self-confidence. All around us, and throughout human history, there are and have been men and women with exceptionally high levels of self-confidence who have gone on to achieve extraordinary things.

In studying the lives and stories of these people, we find that some of them started out with high levels of self-confidence that they learned from their parents in early childhood. However, most of them started off the same way we all start off, with deep-down feelings of inferiority and inadequacy. Because of destructive criticism, lack of love, and other mistakes that parents make with us in early childhood, we grow up with diminished feelings of self-esteem, low self-confidence, and a feeling that, "I'm not good enough," in comparison with others.

With low self-confidence, many people today work extremely hard on the outside to achieve success. However, when they do, deep down inside they feel like "imposters." This so-called "fear of success" is really a feeling of unworthiness that we can't seem to get rid of no matter how much we achieve. Many successful men and women are repeating the line to the Peggy Lee song, "Is That All There Is?" when looking around them at their homes and cars.

You Want to Be Happy

What people want more than anything else is just to feel really good about themselves. We want to be happy and positive and have a sense of well-being. Above all, what we really want is *peace of mind*, and you can only enjoy peace of mind when you feel confident in your ability to deal effectively with the requirements of life, with your family, your friends, your work, your customers, your social activities, and all the other things that you are involved in.

The law of cause and effect tells us that if we want to enjoy the effect of high self-confidence, we need only engage in the causes of high self-confidence. If we can find out what it is that other highly self-confident men and women think and say and do, and then do the same things, we will eventually get the same results. We will eventually feel the same way. We will eventually become unstoppable.

Mental Marathon Training

It's often hard for people to believe that mental qualities can be developed just as physical qualities can be developed. If this were a program on how to run a physical marathon, and I was offering to train you, day by day, over the next six months, to run a marathon, you would come to realize that even a nonrunner can go from being physically unfit to running a marathon of 26.4 miles in six months of disciplined training. Today, there are even men and women in their 50s and 60s who are running marathons with this kind of training.

What this book will do for you is to put you through a "mental marathon." This marathon will not be as arduous or painful physically as a physical marathon, but it will still require a tremendous amount of work. The amount of work that you put in will exactly determine the results that you get out.

If you follow these proven and practical principles, drawn from the lives and behaviors of the most successful men and women alive today, and all of which are scientifically validated by extensive research and experience, you can develop the self-confidence that you desire so that you can achieve anything you really want. Let's begin.

The POWER of SELF-CONFIDENCE

The Foundation of Self-Confidence

There is nothing either good or bad, but thinking makes it so.
—William Shakespeare

Your thoughts and feelings about yourself, and what you can or cannot do, are the sum total result of a lifetime of experience and conditioning, and usually have little relationship to what is truly possible for you.

In personal development, there is a principle, or a law of becoming, that simply says that each person is in a continual process of *becoming*, or evolving and growing, in the direction of his or her dominant thoughts.

Your body is also in a state of becoming. At a normal rate of cell death and replenishment, you have a brand-new body every seven years. Whereas your physical evolution in becoming is effected by the food that you put into your body, your mental evolution and becoming is largely determined by the thoughts that you put into your mind.

You Become What You Think About

The law of concentration says that "anything you dwell upon grows in your reality." Anything that you think about long enough and hard enough eventually becomes a part of your mental processes, exerting its influence and power on your attitude and your behavior.

If you constantly think thoughts of boldness and courage and self-assertion, you become progressively bolder and more courageous and more self-assertive. The more you dwell on the person you would like to be, with the qualities you would like to have, the more you implant those deep into your subconscious mind where they become part of your ongoing evolution. What you habitually think about eventually becomes a part of your character and your personality.

3

In this sense, you are a *self-made* man or woman. You are where you are and what you are because of the thoughts that you have allowed to preoccupy your mind. Whatever you have dwelled on over the past months and years, you have become, and you are, right now, today, the result of all those thoughts.

Not only have you made yourself into the person you are today, but you are continuing with the job of construction with every thought you think. Because this is an unavoidable fact of life, the smartest thing that you can do is to persistently think the thoughts that are consistent with the kind of person you would like to be.

Personal Growth Is Not Easy

However, for most people this is too big a leap. Most people continue to think about and talk about exactly what they *don't* want to happen, and then they are constantly amazed that exactly what they were hoping to avoid happens to them again and again.

One of the most profound discoveries in all of human history is that "thought is creative." *Thoughts held in mind, produce after their kind.* Like begets like. Your thoughts become your realities. You *do* become what you think about most of the time. You cannot harbor one kind of thought and experience a different kind of existence. This law of cause and effect works perfectly, everywhere and always, for everyone.

The development of unshakable self-confidence, therefore, begins with you taking full, complete, systematic and purposeful control of the contents of your conscious mind, disciplining yourself to think consistently about only the things that you desire and to resolutely keep your mind off the things that you fear.

All of life is from the inside out. It is from the inner to the outer. The law of correspondence, perhaps one of the most important of all the mental laws, says that "your outer world will be a reflection of your inner world." What you see on the outside is largely a reflection of what is going on inside you. This is not only true for you; it is true for everyone around you.

Your Inner Life Predicts Your Outer Life

Many times we see people who seem to be very nice and pleasant on the outside, but who seem to have continuous problems in their personal and business lives. We wonder, "How could these unhappy things happen to such nice people?"

The unavoidable fact is that, with few exceptions, most of what a person experiences in his or her outer life corresponds exactly to something that is going on in their inner life, something that you seldom know, and it cannot be otherwise.

True happiness and success comes from living your life in harmony with the laws that govern your being. Even though these laws are invisible, they are like the law of gravity, which is also invisible but is to be violated only at your own peril. Happy people are those who obey and follow the laws of nature and live their lives consistent with those laws.

Start with Your Inner Life

If you want to enjoy self-confidence on the *outside*, you must practice complete integrity on the *inside*. The foundation of self-confidence is for you to live your life consistent with your innermost values and principles, while thinking and acting in harmony with your highest aspirations.

Men and women with the most rock-solid self-confidence are those who are absolutely clear about what it is they believe to be right and good and worthwhile, and who live their lives consistent with these values. Everything they do or say is an expression of their innermost convictions. Your whole world can fall down around you, but as long as you know that you are doing the right thing, you will have a deep inner sense of calm that will manifest itself in an attitude of confidence and self-assurance in any situation.

You will have many ups and downs in life, but what is most important is that you remain "true to yourself." Then, as Shakespeare said, "thou can'st not then be false to any man."

Determine Your Values

The starting point of developing high levels of self-confidence and in becoming a superior human being is for you to think through and to decide on your values. Superior men and women are those who have taken the time to decide clearly what it is they believe in, and in what order, and they have then organized their lives so that everything they do reflects those values.

Recently, I addressed about 150 members of the national sales force of a very successful company. This company had started from an idea and had grown very rapidly in an extremely competitive market, and the company was very profitable.

All the people at the meeting were remarkably positive and upbeat and had a special quality of goodness about them. When I commented on this, the president of the company showed me the value statement that the executives of the company had worked out before they had begun operations.

There were two pages of values and principles that were given to everyone in the company when they began. These two pages had been subsequently reduced onto plasticized cards that each person could carry in their wallet or purse.

The president told me an interesting story. He said that whenever two or more people in the company were wrestling with a decision of any kind, even over the telephone, they would pull out their plasticized cards describing the corporate values. They would then review the values together, one by one, and compare the various options available to them with each value. Whatever decision they finally made would always stand the values test, without question.

Values in Business

In a recent study covering 25 years of business history, the researchers found that the companies that had very clear *written* values to which everyone in the company ascribed had earned an average of 700 percent greater profit over the 25 years than other companies in the same industries that did not have a written codes of values. "As within, so without."

Whenever I conduct a strategic planning exercise for a corporation, the executives of the corporation always select integrity as their highest value and most important organizing principle for the entire corporation.

In my experience, almost every corporation will select the value of integrity as one of their foremost organizing principles. The word *integrity*, according to the dictionary, means "perfect, undivided, complete, unified, a single whole, without blemish or fault." It's a fine value to choose.

This is a good choice, but, in reality, integrity is more than a value. It is the one quality of mind that assures or *guarantees all the other values* that you select.

The economic and personal results of individuals and corporations with clear values always tend to be far superior to those of companies and individuals whose values are vague or unclear.

Clarify Your Personal Values

Your starting point toward higher self-confidence and personal greatness is to, first of all, clarify your values for yourself. It is for you to decide for yourself the values that you believe in. What do you stand for and, even more, what will you not stand for? What values do you espouse that you are willing to sacrifice for? What values would you pay for or sweat for—or maybe even die for?

Do you value your family? Your God? Your health? Your work or career? Do you value principles such as freedom, liberty, compassion for the less fortunate, or "reverence for life?" Do you believe in honesty and truth and sincerity and hard work and success? Whatever your values are, think them through and write them down.

Who Do You Most Admire?

A useful exercise is for you to think of the men and women, living and dead, whom you most admire. What qualities or attributes of these people do you consider the most important? If you could be like any one of these people, which of their qualities would you most want to emulate?

When you look around you at the people you admire, what qualities of these people do you consider the most important? What qualities do you look for in your friends and associates when you are trying to decide whether to become deeply involved with them? What do you think are the fundamental qualities or values that underlie business and personal relationships? What are *your* values?

Values Are Nonnegotiable

When you select a value, if it's to be one of your values at all, it becomes inviolable. Either it is a fixed value and you live every part of your life consistent with it, or it is not one of your values. You cannot have a value when it is convenient and put it aside when it's not convenient. You cannot have a little bit of integrity: It must be all or nothing.

The act of selecting your values is also the act of clearly stating to yourself, and sometimes to others, exactly how you will live your life from this moment forward. Once you have selected a value, and you have declared it to be one of your unifying principles, you are, in effect, saying that this is something on which you will never compromise. And your level of adherence to the values you have personally selected is the real measure of your character, your true quality as a human being.

Unshakable self-confidence comes from unshakable commitment to your values. When, deep down inside yourself you know that you will never violate your highest principles, you experience a deep sense of personal power that enables you to deal openly and honestly and with complete self-confidence in almost every human situation.

Values Clarification

If you're having any difficulty in clarifying your values, a very help-ful exercise is to take some time to write out your own obituary or eulogy. Imagine that everyone you know and care about is gathered at your funeral to pay their last respects. The minister reads your eulogy to this assembly of people, and in it he describes the person you became over the course of your lifetime. He describes not only what you accomplished and what you contributed to the lives of others, but he reads out the virtues, values, and qualities that you were known for by the people around you.

This obituary can become your vision of the kind of person you wish to be and the kind of values that you wish to live by. No one is perfect, and we all have a long way to go in living our lives consistent with our highest values, but the very exercise of writing out your obituary will exert a powerful influence on everything you do thereafter. Both consciously and unconsciously, you will be drawn toward living and acting more and more like the person you described in that final testament.

Organize Your Values

Once you've decided on your values, your work is not over. Now you have to organize your values by priority. You have to decide which value is more important and which value is less important. If you wrote out each of your values on small squares of paper and then you had to throw away all the squares but one, which one would you keep? This then becomes your foremost value, the one that takes precedence over all others.

Which would be your second most important value? Your third? Your fourth? And so on. Your order of priority is extremely important in determining the kind of person you are and the kind of life you live.

Many people organize their values with number one being God, number two being their family, number three being their health, number four being their career, and perhaps number five being success. A person with this order of values is saying that, when push comes to shove, I will always favor the higher-order value over the lower-order value.

Order of Values Forces You to Choose

If your family comes before your health or your work, you would always sacrifice your health or your work for the well-being of your family. If your order of values was changed and your work or financial success came before your health, you would be saying that you would sacrifice your health if that were necessary to get ahead in your career.

I have known businessmen who put career success ahead of their families in their order of priority. When they had to choose one or the other, they regularly chose their work over spending time with their spouse and children. As a result, both the marriages and the careers have run into serious trouble.

Selecting your values and then putting them in order of importance actually creates a mental and emotional structure that enables you to make better choices and decisions in every area of your life.

Integrity Revisited

The principle of integrity, or adherence to your values, seems to be a law of the universe. Whenever you violate or compromise your integrity for anything, there seems to be a great power or force of retribution that will not allow you to get away with it.

Integrity seems to be an absolute requirement for successful human living. A failing in integrity, or compromising your values, not only seems to bring about a punishment that fits the crime, whether it is in business, politics, or personal life, but it seems to create a high level of stress, unhappiness, and inner turmoil in the life of the individual.

This need for absolute integrity seems to require that you "live in truth" with all people and under all circumstances. Living in truth means that you never live a lie. It means that you never compromise your integrity for the sake of a job, or money, or a relationship. It means that you always do and say what you know to be right and true, no matter what the short-term cost or benefit.

Living in truth means that you do not pretend or practice self-delusion. You face life, your relationships, and your circumstances, exactly as they are, not as you wish they would be. Living in truth means that you never stay in a situation that makes you unhappy or which you feel for any reason is wrong for you.

Set Peace of Mind as Your Highest Principle

Living in truth means that you set peace of mind as your highest goal and as your core organizing principle. You select all your other goals to be consistent with it. You never compromise your peace of mind for anyone or anything else.

You do and say only those things that feel perfectly right for you. You accept your own thoughts and feelings completely, whatever they are, and you systematically change each part of your life that is not giving you peace of mind. Only in this way can you enjoy the high levels of self-confidence that are experienced by the superior individual. Only by insisting that everything you do allows you to live in peace with yourself can you feel really terrific about yourself and get along wonderfully in all your relationships.

Your Values Are Only Expressed in Your Actions

Living consistent with your values is the key to happiness, harmony, well-being, and high levels of self-confidence. This brings us to the final point in this chapter, perhaps the most important point of all. It is that your true values are only expressed in your *actions*, in what you do.

You can tell what you truly believe by observing what you do in any situation in which you have to make a choice. Especially when you are under stress, and pulled in two directions at once, with opposing demands or responsibilities, this is when your true values are revealed.

The action that you take in any given situation will tell you which of your values is uppermost or whether you have any values at all. It is not what you say, hope, wish, or intend, but only what you do that counts. Your choices of the actions you take tell you unerringly who you really are.

In fact, you can tell what your values have been in the past by looking back and observing what you did under stress when you had an important choice to make. Did you listen to the "better angels of your nature," or did you compromise for a short-term advantage?

A person who says that his or her family comes first and then has to choose between working late or going to a child's school play or sports activity, and who chooses the child's needs over the boss's requirements, is a person who is living consistent with his or her highest values.

Everyone has had the experience of walking away from a job or a relationship even though considerable sacrifice was involved because it was the right—though painful—thing to do, and you probably remember how great you felt as a result!

Whenever you act consistent with a higher value, you always feel terrific about yourself, and your self-confidence soars. However, whenever you compromise your values for any reason, you feel uncomfortable, inferior, guilty, and your self-confidence plummets.

The Law of Reversibility

The fact that your true values are only expressed in your actions brings us to a little-known mental principle called the law of reversibility. This law says that just as thoughts and feelings lead to actions consistent with them, the principle is reversible, and actions consistent with particular values or beliefs actually lead to the thoughts and feelings that would have triggered the actions.

What this means is that, even if you start off lacking a particular quality, if you deliberately act as if you already have the quality, you will eventually create within yourself the mental quality that corresponds to the action.

Dr. William James of Harvard put it this way, "Action seems to follow feelings, but really action and feelings go together; and by regulating the action, which is under the more direct control of the will, we can indirectly regulate the feeling, which is not."

The Act-As-If Principle

You can develop within yourself a superb set of values by acting as though you *already* had those values. You can develop integrity and courage and compassion and confidence by behaving as though you already had these qualities. The more you "act the part," especially when you demonstrate these qualities under stress or when you feel like doing or saying something else, the more rapidly these qualities become a permanent part of your mental makeup. The more you practice good values, the more rapidly you become a truly superior person.

The keys to developing the unshakable self-confidence that will make everything else possible for you are *self-control, self-mastery,* and *self-discipline.* Self-confidence can come directly, by behaving in a self-confident manner, but more often it comes *indirectly*, by doing and saying the things and practicing the behaviors that lead to self-confidence. The most important self-development behavior is living consistently with your highest values at every opportunity.

The Principle of Resistance

In weight lifting, repetitive lifting of heavy weights develops muscles. The heavier the weight and the greater the resistance, the more blood rushes into the capillaries and the bigger the muscles become.

In mental development, there is a principle of "resistance" as well. In developing "mental muscles," especially the mental muscle or quality of self-confidence, you can use this principle to accelerate your own development. Whenever you exert self-mastery and discipline yourself to do or say the right thing, especially under stress, you create resistance to your natural tendencies. This resistance generates *friction*. This is the same kind of friction, or heat, that, when applied to a crucible containing chemicals, will cause the chemicals to crystallize and take on a new form.

Whenever you create mental friction by resisting your natural tendencies, instead doing what you know is right and true and consistent with your highest values, especially in a difficult situation, the "mental heat" causes your values to crystallize at a higher level and eventually become a permanent part of your character.

Developing Inner Strength

Each human quality is subject to this same formulation. Once you have persisted through great adversity, you are always capable of persisting through lesser difficulties. Once you have acted courageously in a major confrontation, you are always able to act courageously in the face of lesser confrontations. When you behave honestly when there are large amounts at stake, you are always able, later on, to behave honestly when you are dealing with lesser amounts.

The foundation of self-confidence, the basis of boldness and self-assertion, is a deep inner trust, based on living a life of perfect integrity, and disciplining yourself to live consistent with your highest values in every situation. Each time you do this, you will feel positive and happy and wonderful about yourself. Your behaviors will further crystallize in your personality and become a more permanent part of the exceptional human being that you are in the process of becoming.

Action Exercises

1. List your three most important values governing your personal life.

2. List the three most important values that you practice in your work and business life.

3. List the three people, living or dead, who you would most like to spend an afternoon with.

4. Why would you want to spend an afternoon with these people? What would you ask them or talk about?

5. Why would these three people want to spend an afternoon with you? What are your most admirable qualities?

6. List three times where you have lived consistent with your highest values when you could have compromised.

7. What are you going to do differently from now on to assure that your values and actions are in harmony?

CHAPTER 2

Purpose and Personal Power

There can be no great courage where there is no confidence or assurance, and half the battle is in the conviction that we can do what we undertake.

—Orison Swett Marden

The development of unshakable self-confidence will open up such possibilities for you as you cannot now imagine. You will be able to dream bigger dreams, set bigger goals, make greater commitments and plunge into life more wholeheartedly than you ever have before.

Self-confidence is the hinge on which the gate of individual achievement turns. When your self-confidence becomes unlimited, you will be able to realize more of your potential than you could under any other circumstances.

More than 2,000 years ago, Aristotle wrote that "Happiness is a condition. It is not something that is achieved by pursuing it directly, but rather comes as a result of our engaging in purposeful activities."

The Law of Indirect Effort

In a way, this is a restatement of the law of indirect effort. This law states that almost everything we get in life involving people and emotional experiences comes to us more *indirectly* rather than directly. They come to us as a result of doing something else.

For example, if we pursue happiness *directly*, it eludes us. However, if we get busy doing something that is really important to us and begin to make real progress in the direction of our dreams and aspirations, we find ourselves feeling very happy indeed.

Self-confidence is also subject to the law of indirect effort. We achieve higher levels of self-confidence not by wishing for it, but by setting and achieving ever-higher goals and objectives. As we move forward step by step, as we feel ourselves advancing in life, we feel better and stronger and more capable of taking on even bigger challenges.

Become More Confident and Competent

We develop the confidence to tackle larger goals by applying our energies to the accomplishment of smaller goals. We build up our confidence as we move forward until we reach the point at which there is nothing that we won't take on.

In fact, the habit of setting and achieving ever-larger goals is absolutely indispensable to the development of ever-higher levels of self-confidence and personal power. You can only really believe in yourself when you absolutely know that you have the ability to do what you set out to do.

True self-confidence does not come from positive wishing or positive hoping or positive thinking. It comes from positive *knowing* based on having proven to yourself, over and over again, that you have what it takes to get from wherever you are to wherever you want to go.

Self-confidence is a state of mind. It is an attitude and, as an attitude, it is more important than facts. However, it must be based on facts to be the kind of self-confidence you can rely on in a crunch. Your job is to do whatever it takes to convince yourself, in your heart, that you are absolutely *unstoppable* and that you can achieve anything that you put your mind to.

Thought Is Creative

If self-confidence is an attitude of mind, it is based on mental principles and mental laws, foremost of which is, "Thought is creative." You are not what you *think* you are, but what you *think*, you *are*. As you systematically and deliberately change your thinking about yourself, your outer reality changes to conform with it. Your thoughts create your life, including and especially your thoughts with regard to your feelings of self-confidence.

The reason that goals are so important is because of these mental laws, the consequences of which are inevitable and inescapable. You are happy and successful to the degree to which you conform your life and your thinking to these laws, and live in harmony with them.

The first law, which we have already discussed, is the law of cause and effect. This law is so simple and powerful that you need to remind yourself of it all the time. Everything that happens in your life—success or failure, wealth or poverty, health or illness, happiness or unhappiness, self-confidence or insecurity—are all subject to this law.

The Bible teaches this basic law as the principle of "sowing and reaping." It says that "whatsoever a man soweth, that also shall he reap." This especially refers to the thoughts you think. If you sow positive, optimistic, uplifting thoughts in your mind, you will reap positive, optimistic uplifting events and experiences in your life. It cannot be otherwise.

If you sow clear goals and objectives in your mind, you will reap clear results and rewards in your outer life.

The Law of Attraction

A corollary of the law of cause and effect is the law of attraction. This is one of the most important of all mental laws in explaining what happens to you. This law says that like attracts like.

It says that you inevitably attract into your life the people, ideas, circumstances, and opportunities that are in harmony with your dominant thoughts. Just like a magnet attracts iron filings, you attract whatever is consistent with whatever you are thinking about most of the time.

Because this is a law, you cannot think one thing and attract something else. Whatever you are thinking about most of the time you are drawing into your life from all directions. This is why "fuzzy" goals bring "fuzzy" results. Clear goals bring clear results. Because your level of self-confidence is directly tied to how effective you feel you are in achieving your goals, it is very important that you know exactly what it is you want and that you think of nothing else.

The Law of Correspondence

Another mental law, also a corollary of the law of cause of effect, is the law of correspondence. This law says that your outer world tends to correspond to your inner world. Your outer world of health, wealth, and relationships will be a reflection of the way you think about each of these subjects.

There is a saying that "thoughts held in mind produce after their kind." Your thoughts and goals are like seeds, and your mind is like fertile soil. Whatever seeds, positive or negative, clear or unclear, you are planting into your mind will grow in your reality.

Whatever you are reaping or experiencing today is the result of what you have sown in the past. Since your mind is not a vacuum, it doesn't remain empty. Like a garden, either flowers or weeds will grow.

Your thoughts are the most powerful forces in your universe. They are both creative and causative. Every minute of every day, they are forming the world around you. As Shakespeare said, "Nothing is, but thinking makes it so." Your life is what your thoughts make it.

The Law of Concentration

Another principle that affects you life is called the law of concentration. This is an important principle in determining the development and maintenance of your self-confidence. The law of concentration, as mentioned earlier, says that whatever you dwell on continually grows in your reality.

Thinking about a subject, dwelling on it continually, is like watering and fertilizing a seed. Concentration causes it to grow faster in your experience. The more you dwell on any goal or subject, the more of your mental capacities are dedicated to making that goal or subject a reality.

The law of concentration explains why unwavering dedication to a single purpose goes hand-in-hand with all great accomplishment. The ability to concentrate without diversion on a single subject, to the exclusion of all others, explains why ordinary people achieve extraordinary things. Peter Drucker once said that whenever you find something getting done, you find a "monomaniac with a mission."

Because of this mental law, when an average individual with average capabilities brings all of his or her mental powers to bear on the achievement of a single goal, often far more can be accomplished than a seemingly more fortunate person whose energies are dispersed by having several goals at once, or as quite commonly happens, no goals at all.

The Law of Substitution

The law of substitution states that "your conscious mind can only hold one thought at a time, positive or negative." Whatever thought is held continuously in your conscious mind will eventually be accepted by your subconscious mind as an instruction or command.

Your subconscious mind, in harmony with these other mental laws, will go to work 24 hours per day to bring your dominant thought or idea into reality. Your subconscious mind is inordinately powerful. It is the repository of all your emotions, beliefs, values, attitudes, and feelings. All your thoughts and feelings throughout life are stored in your subconscious.

The development of the unshakable self-confidence that you desire requires that you step up to your "mental computer" and take every step necessary to *program* self-confidence deep into your subconscious mind.

The Law of Emotion

The final mental law you need to know in the development of purpose, personal power, and self-confidence is the law of emotion. This law says that every decision that you make, every thought you think, every action you take, is based on an emotion of some kind. The two primary emotions are either the emotion of *fear*, at one end of the spectrum of emotions, or the emotion of *desire*, at the other end of the spectrum.

When you hold an emotion-charged thought in your conscious mind, it is rapidly accepted by your subconscious. Your subconscious then activates all your mental powers and begins to turn that inner thought into a result or experience in your outer world.

The more powerful the emotion—the more affect it has on your thinking and actions—the more rapid the change in your experience. If the emotion is strong enough, the change can be instantaneous.

The Power of Decision

I had a friend who smoked for 30 years. He claimed that he couldn't quit smoking because it was a deeply entrenched habit, going back to early adulthood. One day he had some chest pains and went to his doctor, who performed a series of tests on him. When the results of the tests were in, the doctor sat my friend down and told him that he had a serious heart condition and that if he continued to smoke, he would be dead within six months.

Samuel Johnson once said, "When a man is to be hanged on the morrow, it clears his mind wondrously." The idea of dying was so emotionally charged to my friend that he took out his cigarettes, threw them in the wastebasket, and never touched one again.

In a positive vein, if you are absolutely convinced that you are meant to be a great success in life, and that there was nothing in the world that could stop you from achieving great things as long as you threw yourself wholeheartedly into every activity, and persisted until you succeeded, you would become an irresistible force of nature. The depth of your belief and the strength of your conviction would dramatically increase the power of your personality. If you really believed in your ability to succeed greatly, you would become unstoppable.

The Four Cs of Inner Confidence

You can develop this kind of belief, this inner confidence, by developing what I call "the four Cs."

1. **Clarity:** Decide exactly what it is you want to accomplish and exactly the kind of person you wish to become.

2. **Conviction:** Develop the unshakable belief that you can do anything that you can put your mind to.

3. **Commitment:** Resolve to do whatever is necessary; develop the willingness to pay the price, in advance, for any success you desire.

4. **Consistency:** Resolve to work on your goals every day, morning, noon, and night, until they are accomplished.

When you back your goals and actions with clarity, conviction, commitment, and consistency, you are on your way to developing the kind of confidence that will make everything possible for you.

The Importance of Goals

The reason goals are so important in the development of self-confidence is because the very act of setting a major goal for your life activates all the mental laws in your favor. It will be as though all the switches were flipped on in your engine of accomplishment, and the after-burners were turned on to your potential.

Clear goals free you from the law of accident, the tendency for things to happen in a random and unpredictable way. Goals give you a clear sense of direction and the knowledge that your life is self-determined. Goals give you a sense of power, purpose, and focus. They make you feel that everything that happens to you is part of an organized plan that is taking you, step by step, toward the attainment of your highest ideals.

Your ability to set goals and to make plans for their accomplishment is the "master skill" of success, without which very little is possible. The habit of regular goal-setting and goal-achieving is probably more important than any other skill you could ever learn.

The Master Skill of Success

Over the years, I have personally witnessed thousands of examples among my students of the amazing powers of goal setting. Recently,

I addressed about 600 members of a national association at their annual convention in Phoenix, Arizona. During this talk, I emphasized the importance of writing down exactly what it was they wanted, and then making written plans to accomplish it.

That was on a Saturday. About five days later, on the following Thursday, one of the attendees called my office to get my fax number. He said he wanted to send something immediately and didn't want to wait for the mail.

The letter that came in told this amazing story: the gentleman who wrote said that he had heard about goal setting many times and that he was prepared to be unimpressed with the talk that I gave at the convention. However, exactly the opposite happened. He decided to sit down after the convention and seriously write out his goals for the following year.

The letter went on to say that on Sunday he made out a list of 10 goals, both personal and financial, that he wanted to accomplish over the next 12 months. What astonished him was that he had accomplished 5 of the 10 goals by Monday, the next day, at 5 o'clock. He could hardly believe it! He quickly wrote down 5 more goals, to bring his list for the year back up to 10, and by Thursday, when he wrote this letter, he had accomplished 5 more of his new list of 10 goals. He felt that he had made more progress in a week with clear, written goals and plans than he had made in the previous year.

Remarkable Success Stories

Another gentleman, a recent immigrant from Pakistan, was dead broke and sleeping on the ground when someone tried to help him by letting him listen to an audio program of mine on goal setting. It transformed his life. Four years later, he had started and built two successful businesses and was worth more than a million dollars.

A woman who was going through a difficult period of her life, with personal, health, and financial problems, decided to sit down and set some new goals and make some plans to resolve her difficulties. As a result, within one year, she got out of a bad relationship, joined Alcoholics Anonymous and quit drinking, lost 40 pounds, and tripled her income to more than a $100,000 per year. She attributed her successes to the power of written goals.

There are countless other testimonies to the power of written goals. I receive them in person and via e-mail every week, from people all over the world. Before this chapter is finished, I will give you a simple goal-setting technique that can put your life into overdrive.

Fear Holds You Back

Remember when I said that everything that you do is the result of either fear or desire? Fear is, and has always been, the greatest enemy of mankind, and it is also the greatest enemy of self-confidence. It is fear that holds us back more than any other factor. Fear, of all kinds, works on us unconsciously to undermine and sabotage our best intentions and our greatest hopes.

In fact, as you read these words, you are probably thinking of a fear that holds you back in some way. No matter what you do, fear will rear its ugly head and attempt to trip you up. Sometimes, the fear will appear consciously in the form of rationalizations and excuses that you use to sabotage yourself and hold yourself back.

Sometimes, you will find yourself avoiding goal setting by saying that "I already know what my goals are; I don't need to write them down." Your subconscious will tell you, "If you don't set any clear goals, you can't fail." This is just another way of saying that you don't really believe in your ability to do any better than you are doing right now.

Fear will often appear as procrastination about writing down your goals in the first place. You'll resolve to write out your goals and plans on the weekend, or on your vacation, or during the summertime, or when you can dedicate a few hours to it, or sometime in the indefinite future. Then, like 97 percent or more of adults, you'll never do it.

You will start to rationalize and say, "Well, considering my situation, it probably wouldn't make any difference anyway."

The Comfort Zone

If the greatest enemy of self-confidence is fear, then the greatest enemy of human achievement is the *comfort zone*. Psychologists have determined that each of us has natural tendency to slip into a zone of performance and behavior where we are comfortable, one that is easy and unchallenging, and then to stay there.

We stop striving. We relax. And day-by-day, we develop the habits that lead to underachievement and failure. We settle for far less than we're truly capable of. We engage in social networking, watch television, listen to music, socialize, and generally waste our time, and then we eventually convince ourselves that this is the very best that we can do.

Most people are in comfort zones of their own making. Your attitude and personality, your habitual way of responding to people and to life, is your comfort zone. The amount you earn, your standard of living, and your level of performance in your work is your comfort zone. Your level of mental and physical fitness is your comfort zone.

Resistance to Change

The natural tendency, once a person gets into a comfort zone, is to resist change of any kind, even beneficial change. If you are forced out of your comfort zone, like the collapse of a relationship, or the loss of a job, your natural tendency will be to attempt to recreate the same comfort zone, with the same type of person, or doing the same work.

Everyone has had the experience of losing a job that they disliked only to go out looking for a similar job, doing the same work. We get into a relationship that doesn't work out and our natural tendency is to try to form a new relationship with a similar type of person. We earn a certain amount of money and rather than striving to increase our earning ability, we adjust our lifestyle and accommodate to our financial situation.

The tragedy of the comfort zone is that it, first of all, starts off by being comfortable, but it leads rapidly to complacency.

Complacency eventually leads to boredom, to the question, "Is this all there is?" Instead of life being an exciting adventure, it becomes merely a boring repetition of what happened yesterday.

Eventually, the comfort zone leads through complacency and boredom to frustration and unhappiness. Deep down inside, the average person knows that he or she is put on this earth with amazing capabilities. He or she knows that there is something better than this. As Carl Rogers, the psychologist, once said, "There is within every organism an inborn drive toward the complete fulfillment of its inherent possibilities." There is a nagging "something" inside that tells each person that there is far more that he or she could be and have and do. This feeling is within you as well.

The Attainment of Personal Greatness

Great men and women are those who absolutely believe that they are put on this earth to do something wonderful with their lives. They have a vision of something greater or better than their current circumstances. Personal greatness means having a sense of destiny and a conviction that your thoughts and your imagination are the only real limits to your possibilities.

William James said, "Compared to what we ought to be, we are only half awake. We are making use of only a small part of our physical and mental resources. Stating the thing broadly, the human individual thus lives far within his limits. He possesses powers of various sorts which he habitually fails to use."

The founder of *Success* magazine, Orison Swett Marden, once said, "There are powers inside of you, which, if you could discover and use, would make of you everything you ever dreamed or imagined you could become."

In a five-year study of leaders, reported on in his book, "Leaders," Warren Bennis discovered that each of them consciously avoided the "comfort zone" by continuously setting higher goals. They never allowed themselves to become complacent. They lived their lives fully extended, always striving to be and do more.

To develop unshakable self-confidence, you need to see yourself and think of yourself as a *leader*, and to do what leaders do. You need to stretch yourself toward the outermost boundaries of your potential. You need to set goals that draw out of you the very best that is in you. You need to work toward objectives that cause you to feel a sense of mastery and peak performance. And it all begins with a pad of paper, a pen, and you.

Imagine No Limitations

The starting point of setting goals is for you to throw off all mental limitations and let your mind roam freely across the entire universe of possibilities. Your primary job at the beginning is to allow yourself to "dream big dreams" and determine exactly what it is you want out of life, in every area and in every dimension. Decide what's right before you decide what's possible. Imagine that you can be or have or do virtually anything that you really want to, as long as you know exactly what it is.

First, make up a *dream list*. Temporarily imagine that you have no limitations of time, money, knowledge, contacts, experience, or education. Imagine that anything that you can write down is possible for you. Remember, anything that you can clearly define and crystallize on paper is probably possible, if you want it long enough and hard enough and are willing to make whatever efforts and sacrifices are necessary.

There are no unrealistic goals, only unrealistic *timelines*. The very act of writing your goals down sets the whole universe to work in your favor, and activates all the mental laws to help you. In fact, many people have had the experience of writing out a list of goals on New Year's Day, putting them away and not referring to them again until the end of the year, and then finding that 80 percent of the goals have been achieved, sometimes in the most amazing ways.

The very act of writing down big, challenging goals causes three things to happen. First, your self-concept improves and your self-confidence goes up immediately. The act of setting goals requires self-confidence and simultaneously builds self-confidence. Having the courage to write down what you really want improves your self-image and raises your self-esteem. The action itself generates a feeling of greater personal power and ability.

Second, tap into your mental and emotional powers. Goal-setting actually gives you a burst of physical and mental energy. Your heart rate and your respiratory rate speed up. The very act of goal-setting is inherently exciting. It sounds a little corny, but someone once said, "Feeling listless? Make a list!" It's true. It's like stepping on the accelerator of your own mental and physical potential. And if you do it every day, the results can be amazing.

Third, commit it to paper. The very fact that you have committed a goal to paper dramatically increases the likelihood that you will achieve that goal. Your mind is structured in such a way that you cannot write down a goal clearly on paper (not on a computer screen!) without simultaneously having the ability to somehow attain it. The most important question is: "How badly do you want it?"

There are several mental exercises that you use to set your goals:

1. Imagine that you have just won a million dollars cash, and that you can do or have anything you want with the money. What would you do first? Where would you go? What changes would you make in your life? If you had complete financial freedom, what would you do differently from what you are doing now?

2. Describe your ideal lifestyle. Imagine that you could live your ideal of the perfect life. What part of the country would you choose to live in? What kind of a company would you choose to work for or to start and run as your own? What kind of a home and car would you want? How would you like to spend your time and live your life? What kind of relationships would you want?

3. Ask yourself what you would do if you learned today that you only had six months to live. If you had no limitations, how would you spend your last six months on earth? This is another way of asking, "What is really important to you?" Who would you want to spend time with?

What would you want to accomplish? What would you like to leave behind? In other words, what do you truly value? What are the things that really give meaning and purpose to your life?

4. List all the worries or problems in your life and write out a goal that is the perfect solution to each of those difficulties. If money is a concern, write out a goal that clearly defines how much you want to earn, how much you want to accumulate, and what you want to achieve financially over the next three to five years.

5. Think about your family and your relationships. Describe the perfect situation between you and the important people in your life, and then make out a series of goals to achieve that situation.

6. Look at your health. Describe what perfect health and physical fitness means to you, and then make out a plan to achieve that level of fitness.

7. Define the kind of person that you would most like to become, both personally and professionally. Then, work out a plan of personal and professional development that will enable you to learn and grow and become the kind of person you most admire and would most like to be. Remember, as Goethe said, "Before you can have something, you must first be something."

Categorize Your Goals

Once you have written out your goals, divide them into the different areas of your life that are important. There are basically six divisions that most people use, but you can have more or fewer.

1. Financial and material goals.
2. Family and personal goals.
3. Self-improvement and educational goals.

4. Spiritual goals.
5. Health and fitness goals.
6. Social and community goals.

To perform at your very best, your life must be in balance. This means that you need to have goals in each area so that you are moving progressively forward on something that is important to you all the time.

Organize Your Goals

The next step, once you have all your goals in writing, is to organize them in order of *priority*. Select the goals that are more important than others and put them at the top of each list. Then, select the goals that are second and third and fourth, and so on.

Finally, and perhaps the most important of all in goal setting, is for you to select the one goal out of all the goals that is more important than any other. This is the key to your success. The mental discipline to set your goals and to sort them out, and to decide on your chief aim or your *major definite purpose*, is the starting point of individual greatness.

This major definite purpose is the one goal, the accomplishment of which will lead to the attainment of many of your other goals. This goal becomes the central focus for all your other goals and activities. This goal is what enables you to bring all your mental resources to focus like a laser beam on one thing. Your forward progress on this one goal is what eventually generates the unshakable self-confidence that you desire.

Focus and Concentrate

This intense focus on one goal is not easy, but it is all-important. Orison Swett Marden wrote, "The giants of the race have been men and women of *concentration*, who have struck sledge-hammer blows in one place until they have accomplished their purpose.

The successful men and women of today are those of one over-mastering idea, one unwavering aim, men and women of single and intense purpose."

Marden also said that "every great man has become great, every successful man has succeeded in proportion as he has confined his powers to one particular channel."

Single-minded concentration in the direction of your dreams will intensify your desires and increase your emotional drive toward your goal. This intensity of concentration will activate the law of attraction and begin to attract people and opportunities into your life to help you to achieve your goal. The more you think about your goal, the more it will come to dominate and direct your life. The more you think about it, the more rapidly you will move toward it and it will move toward you.

Make It Measurable and Bound by Time

Your major goal must be measurable. It's a basic rule that "what gets measured, gets done." Make it clear and quantitative and objective, and, if necessary, break it down into smaller parts that you can work on, one at a time.

Your major goal must also be clearly bound by time. Set a deadline on it. Select a realistic but challenging date for its completion and write it down. If it's a long-term goal, such as two or three years, break it down into smaller parts, with minor goals or benchmarks, every 30 to 60 days.

Create a structure of rewards that you will give yourself on the attainment of each part of your goal, and on the attainment of your entire goal. For maximum motivation and high achievement, you need to tie each goal to a reward and each part of the goal to a smaller reward.

The reward may be dinner out or a vacation or holiday. It may be a new car or a new home. It may be something that affects all the members of your family. Many people enlist the support and cooperation of their spouses and children by agreeing to rewards that everyone will get when the goal is attained. Rewards make the process more fun and interesting, and they act as an inner drive that propels you forward when the going gets rough.

Make Your Plans

Once you have determined your major and minor goals, you construct your plans by making detailed lists of everything that you will have to do to achieve each goal, and then organizing the lists by time and priority.

What will you do first, what will you do second? What is more important? What is less important? Make each activity measurable and put a deadline on it. Select the very first thing that comes to your mind to do, and get started. By setting goals, making plans, and getting started, you will join the top 3 percent of adults in the world today and your success will be virtually guaranteed.

A final point with regard to goals is this: keep your goals *confidential.* You build confidence and personal strength by keeping your goals inside of you and by channeling your efforts purposefully each hour and each day toward their attainment.

Many people make the mistake of talking too much about their goals. Too much talking causes their energies to dissipate and their motivation to decline. It weakens their resolve. They lose the force and the power they would have had if they kept their goals to themselves and instead concentrated on purposeful activities.

A Simple Technique

Let me now give you a simple technique that has transformed my life and the life of almost every person who has ever used it. It is simply this: get yourself a spiral notebook, the kind used in school for taking notes. Begin each day by sitting down with this notebook and writing out your main goals in the *present tense*, as though they were already a reality.

Use strong, definite words like, "I earn," "I achieve," or "I am." You can write other things in this notebook if you like, but the most important action is that you take five minutes each day to write and rewrite your major goals, without referring back to what you wrote yesterday.

Hand writing your goals is called a "psychoneuromotor activity." Each time you write out your goals, you drive them deeper into your subconscious mind. You increase the intensity of your desire and the depth of your belief. You activate the mental laws of concentration and attraction and correspondence. You focus your mental powers and increase your confidence that the goal is achievable.

By rewriting your goals every day, they become clearer and stronger and take on a power of their own. This exercise impresses your goals so deeply into your subconscious mind that they will eventually "lock on," and you will begin to move irresistibly and unstoppably toward their achievement. When this happens, your future will be guaranteed.

As you develop this ability to set and achieve whatever it is you want in life, you will develop the kind of confidence that comes from positive "knowing" rather than positive thinking. You will become unstoppable.

Action Exercises

1. Decide today exactly what you want in life. Set your goals as if you had no limitations, and whatever you wrote, you could achieve.

2. Make a list of 10 goals that you would like to achieve in the next 12 months or so.

3. Write your goals in the present, positive, personal tense. For example, you could write, "I earn $XXX,XXX by this date." This is personal, positive, and in the present tense.

4. Set deadlines on each of your goals, and set subdeadlines if necessary.

5. Make a list of everything you will have to do to achieve your goal and organize the list by sequence and priority. This now becomes your plan.

6. Review your list and ask, "If I could be guaranteed to achieve any one goal on my list within 24 hours, which one goal would have the greatest positive impact on my life?"

7. Take this number-one goal, your major definite purpose, write it at the top of a new page in the present, personal, positive tense. Make a list of everything you could do to achieve this goal, organize it into a plan, and take action on your plan immediately.

8. Do something every day, seven days per week on your major goal. Resolve to persist on this goal until you succeed, no matter how hard it becomes or how much time it takes.

This process of setting and achieving one big goal will build your self-confidence to the point where you will become unstoppable for the rest of your life.

CHAPTER 3

Achieving Competence
and Personal Mastery

The quality of a person's life is in direct proportion to their commitment to excellence, no matter what their chosen field.
—Vince Lombardi

You will only be happy, satisfied, and capable of enjoying high levels of self-confidence when you know that you are absolutely excellent at doing something that is important to yourself and others. What is it? What could it be? These are two of the great questions of life.

Fortunately, you and every other person has the inborn ability to become excellent at what you do, and to achieve peak performance in your life and in your chosen field. You have the capacity to function in the "exceptional" range and to achieve mastery in any area that is important to you. The development of lasting self-confidence requires nothing less.

The Edge of the Envelope

In the world of test pilots and prototype aircraft, as described in the book and the movie *The Right Stuff* by Tom Wolfe (Farrar, Straus & Giroux, 1979), they refer continually to what is called the "envelope."

This "envelope" consists of an upper and lower edge. The upper edge marks the height and speed that any previous aircraft or jet has flown, up to the time of the most current test run. This upper edge of the "envelope" is the maximum height and speed deemed possible for a new aircraft before it theoretically comes apart in the air or malfunctions or self-destructs.

The goal of the test pilot is to expand the edge of the envelope. His job is to fly ever faster and higher in order to discover the outer limits of speed, height, and endurance that a particular aircraft is capable of achieving. The test pilot continually takes the aircraft higher and faster until he feels that the plane has reached its absolute outer limits. This is where and when he pulls back to avoid destroying the aircraft, and even fatally crashing.

This is called the "outer edge of the envelope" and it then becomes the "lower edge of the envelope" for the next aircraft and the next round of testing.

Every aircraft, no matter how well made, has an outer limit on its capabilities. It can fly only so fast and so high, and no further. Very little can be done to expand the mechanical ability of something made of metal by the hands of man.

Expand Your Envelope

The major difference between you and an aircraft is that there is no "outer edge" to your personal envelope. As Emerson said, "The power which resides in man is new in nature, and none but he knows what that is which he can do, nor does he know until he has tried."

Thomas Edison said, "If we all did the things we are capable of doing, we would literally astound ourselves." Maxwell Maltz, the author of "Psycho-Cybernetics," said, "Within you right now is the power to do things you never dreamed possible. And this power becomes available to you just as soon as you can change your beliefs."

In other words, the outer limit of *your* envelope, or the outer limit of your potential, is not fixed in time or space, like that of an aircraft. Your limits are determined solely by your own beliefs and by your own confidence in what you think is possible for you.

Self-Confidence and Self-Esteem

Your self-confidence is closely connected to your self-esteem, and to "how much you like yourself." Dr. Nathaniel Brandon calls self-esteem "your reputation with yourself." It is how you feel about yourself and your abilities, in relation to any situation, that determines how much you like yourself and consider yourself to be a valuable and worthwhile person. The more you like yourself, the better you do.

The flip side of self-esteem is what psychologists call "self-efficacy." Self-efficacy is a measure of how effective and competent you feel you are to perform a particular task or to achieve your goals.

This is called "performance-based self-esteem." What this means is that if your self-confidence and your belief in yourself are determined by your self-esteem or how much you like yourself, then your self-esteem is determined by how capable you feel you are in any given set of circumstances.

For example, if a problem comes up at work or home and you are so familiar with it that you can solve it quickly and correctly, your self-efficacy and your self-esteem goes up. You feel more capable and confident and more willing to take on other challenges and difficulties. You feel more positive and optimistic. You feel like an excellent person.

If, on the other hand, a problem or difficulty came up and you were unable to do anything to solve it, and you felt frustrated or ineffective, your self-esteem would suffer and your self-confidence would go down. You would feel negative about yourself and your abilities. You might even become angry or depressed. You would feel powerless rather than powerful.

That's why they say, in playing poker, "The winners laugh and tell jokes while the losers say, 'shut up and deal.'"

Build Your Own Self-Confidence

The law of cause and effect applies to everything you are today and to everything that you become. If the effect that you desire is high and unshakable levels of self-confidence, then it is necessary that you engage in the same behaviors practiced by others who enjoy high and unshakable levels of self-confidence, and you will soon experience high levels of self-confidence yourself.

Studies conducted on thousands of men and women who have moved from ordinary to extraordinary performance, and who have moved from feelings of inadequacy to feeling great about themselves, show that there is a direct cause-effect relationship between competence and mastery on the one hand, and self-confidence on the other.

Mihaly Csikszentmihalyi of the University of Chicago wrote an excellent book, *Flow: The Psychology of Optimal Experience* (Harper

Perennial Modern Classics, 2008). Peak experience is a form of "natural high" that causes you to feel absolutely terrific about yourself, and it gives you a wonderful overall feeling of well-being and happiness. The causes of this effect are now well known.

Achieving Peak Performance

To attain this wonderful, healthy feeling of optimal performance, you need clear goals, challenging standards, regular feedback, total concentration, step-by-step success, and a feeling that you are expanding your capabilities to a new, higher level.

When you have created a situation in which you experience all of these, you sense that you are working at the outer edge of your own personal envelope. You feel that you are getting progressively better and better at something you are ideally suited to do, and that while you are still working within the range of your capabilities, you are stretching yourself at every moment.

When you are caught up in this kind of experience, you often lose track of time. You become unaware of hunger, thirst, or fatigue. You feel calm and clear-headed and euphoric. Tests show when you are in this state of *flow*, your brain releases endorphins, nature's happy drug, which causes you to feel happy and energized.

Often, while you are in this state, the rest of the world seems to slow down. You seem to function with extraordinary clarity. You seem capable of accomplishing great quantities of work in a shorter period of time, with great accuracy and few mistakes. You realize that if you could have this flow experience on a regular basis, you could do incredible things in your work and in your life.

Getting Into the Flow Experience

Everyone has had this heightened experience at some time, usually when they have been under a tremendous amount of stress to get a lot done in a short period of time. However, at the same time, they had clear goals and a strong belief that they were capable of meeting the challenge. At this point, they kicked into "flow" and felt as though they had taken off and left the ground.

You have had this experience yourself in the past. Often, it was so extraordinary that you remembered it for many months or even years. And here's the point. Men and women who achieve extraordinary things in life are merely ordinary men and women who have learned how to put themselves into "flow" and to function at peak performance more often than the average person. And what someone else has done, you can do too.

In every study of success and self-confidence, in every situation in which a person enjoys high levels of self-esteem, self-respect, and personal pride, we find that they all have one thing in common. And that one thing is that each high-achieving man or woman is in the right place, at the right time, doing exactly the work that he or she is uniquely qualified to do. Not only are these people the happiest and highest-performing men and women in our society, but you *personally* will never be truly happy and truly satisfied until you take your rightful place among them.

Find Your True Place

One of the greatest joys of human existence is to find your "true place," the job or occupation that is ideally meant for you, and then to throw your whole heart into doing it and doing it well. The most fortunate people in our society are those who are so totally absorbed in their work that they don't know where their work ends and their play begins. If they could, many of them would do what they love for free, and many do. If they won 10 million dollars in the lottery, this is what they would consciously choose to do for the rest of their lives or until the money ran out.

Spiritual teacher Emmet Fox referred to this as your "heart's desire." He said that you are here on Earth to do something special, something that perhaps only you can do, and that you will never be truly fulfilled until you find it and completely commit yourself to it.

The remarkable thing, said Fox, is that you almost always have an idea of what it is. You only need to listen to yourself, and then trust the guidance you receive.

Grandma Moses

When Grandma Moses, as she came to be called, was a young farm girl, she had a desire to paint, but her family and friends told her that that was nonsense. They told her that, as a farm girl, her role in life was to marry a farm boy and to have and raise farm kids. So she put her heart's desire aside and did what she thought she was supposed to do.

She had children by the time she was out of her teens, and more children in her 20s. In her 40s she became a grandmother, and in her 60s a great-grandmother. When she turned 75, her husband was dead and her children were grown, and the doctor told her that she was too old to work on the farm any longer. She felt that she didn't have much time left, so she decided to fulfill her "heart's desire" and do some painting before she passed on.

She went to a nearby town and visited an art store. The person in the art store sold her some paints and canvasses and brushes, and showed her how to use them. She went back to her farm and sat down and began painting what came to be called "primitive American landscapes."

Grandma Moses finished her first painting when she was 78. When she was one 101 years old, a major gallery in New York City held a showing of her works. In the last 10 years of her life, some of her paintings were selling for more than a $100,000 each.

Now, here's the rub. She was told as a young girl that she couldn't paint because it cost too much and no one could afford it. Yet, when she began painting, she earned more in a year from her paintings than she and her husband had earned in an entire lifetime of hard work on the farm. She was not only a complete natural; she was also a totally original talent.

It's been estimated that, if she had begun painting in her late teens as she really wanted to do, and her paintings had been as successful commercially as they still are today, she might have become one of the richest women in America.

Follow Your Heart

The history of the human race is written in the life stories of men and women who followed their heart's desires and did what they were uniquely qualified to do, and did it with all their heart. And no matter what your situation, this possibility lies open to you, right now.

Colonel Harland Sanders was 66 years old before he sold his first chicken based on his Kentucky Fried Chicken recipe. He had been working as a cook as the owner of his own small café, all his life, preparing fried chicken with his recipe. Then, at the age of 66, when he started doing what he should have been doing decades before, he began building his franchise business and became one of the best known and wealthiest people in the world.

A young man, 16 years old, one of my students, became so excited about his potential, that he started his own food-service business, made a success of it, and sold it out at a profit by the time he was 18 years old. His accomplishment and his confidence as a result were so impressive, that when he went to work for a major grocery chain, they promoted him up the ladder so fast that, before the end of his 18th year, he became the youngest full manager of a major grocery store in America. And he loves every minute of his work.

Courage and Confidence Are Essential

Countless men and women have written to me and returned to my seminars around the country, and they have told me that summing up the courage to do what they really wanted to do was the turning point in their lives. Some of them had dramatically increased their incomes, 5 and 10 times, although many had not. In every case, they were working harder than ever before, but as a result, they were happier than they had ever been. Their postures are strong and straight, their eyes shine, their voices are clear, their language is positive, and it's obvious that they are really enjoying their lives. They have a calm, quiet confidence in themselves that is unmistakable, and it makes them stand out from others around them.

Your development of competence and mastery, and the self-confidence that goes with it, actually begin with self-analysis and self-awareness. Socrates said that the beginning of all wisdom and understanding is contained in the words: "Man, know thyself." In analyzing yourself to determine what it is that would be ideal for you to do, there are six approaches you can use.

First, ask yourself these questions:

1. What talents, skills, and abilities do you have that seem to be natural to you?
2. What have you been able to do easily and well in the past that seems to be difficult for other people?
3. What subjects in school and what parts of your work have you naturally gravitated toward?
4. What did you most enjoy doing between the ages of 7 and 14? (Ask your mother!) This is often a predictor of what you should be doing as an adult.
5. What parts of your work do you love to do and seem to do well?
6. What work or activities give you a natural high? They give you energy, fill you with enthusiasm, and you lose track of time when you are doing them.

Every person is put on this earth with a unique combination of talents and inclinations that makes him or her different from anyone else who has ever lived. And it only is when you find the special situation that can most benefit from your unique capabilities that you will be able to make the greatest contribution and enjoy the great rewards, both tangible and intangible. Finding the right job for you, and then becoming excellent at that job, is one of the chief responsibilities of adult life.

The Four Quadrants of Work

An excellent exercise in self-discovery is for you to divide your work activities into four quadrants. (This was first suggested by Victor Frankl, the founder of logotherapy.) The four quadrants are divided by what is hard to learn versus what is easy to learn and what is hard to do versus what is easy to do.

QUADRANT ONE	**QUADRANT TWO**
Hard to learn; hard to do	*Easy to learn; hard to do*
QUADRANT THREE	**QUADRANT FOUR**
Hard to learn; easy to do	*Easy to learn; easy to do*

Quadrant One: In the first quadrant you find those jobs and activities that are hard to learn and hard to do. These are probably areas for which you have no natural facility and from which you get very little pleasure. Like a sales person having to do detailed account reports or financial analysis, or a computer programmer expected to make sales calls or do public speaking. The individual and the occupation are not suited to each other. They are hard to learn and always hard to do.

Quadrant Two: This quadrant contains things that are easy to learn but hard to do. Hard physical labor might fall into this category, like digging a ditch with a shovel. It's easy to learn, but it's always hard to do.

Quadrant Three: This quadrant contains those jobs or activities that are hard to learn, but easy to do. Driving a car or typing with a typewriter might fall into this category. They are difficult to learn at first, but once you have learned them, they are easy to do afterwards.

Quadrant Four: This quadrant, in terms of what you should ideally be doing, is the most important. These are the jobs that are easy to do and they were so easy to learn that you often forgot how you learned them at all. These are invariably the types of jobs or the kind of work at which you excel and which are almost effortless for you, although they may be difficult for others. This is the work or job that you should be doing with your life.

Examine Your Work History

Look back over your life and ask yourself, "What activities, behaviors, or decisions have been most responsible for my success in life, to date?"

You will probably find that less than 5 percent of the things that you have said or done have accounted for most of the success you have enjoyed. You may find that it was your unique ability to solve a particular kind of problem or to take advantage of a particular type of opportunity. You may find that your special talent was an interpersonal skill that enabled you to influence and persuade other people at a particular time and place. You may find, on analysis, that it was an ability to take charge and accept responsibility for accomplishing a particular goal.

Whatever has been responsible for your successes in life to date may be a good indication what you should be doing in the future.

Design Your Ideal Work Life

Describe in detail the amount of money you would like to earn, the kind of work you would like to do, the size and character of the company you would like to work for, the type of people you would like to work with, the kind of customers that you would like to sell to, and the level of responsibility or position you would like to attain. As you think through the kind of job that would make you happy, you may find that it is a completely different field than the one you are in now.

A woman who was working as an accounting clerk at a computer sales company in New Jersey noticed how much the salespeople were earning and decided that she wanted to get into telephone sales herself. When she applied for the job, she was told that the two occupations, selling and accounting, were totally different, and that a person from accounting had very little probability of success in selling. Nevertheless, she kept asking for a chance to try selling, and, finally, she was given a chance to replace a salesman who was on vacation.

Today, the company sells more than $17,000,000 per year in software and computer peripherals, largely over the phone. This woman is so good at selling that she accounts for more than 50 percent of the total revenues. She went from earning $2,500 per month, to almost half a million dollars per year. Best of all, she has never been happier in her whole life.

Maximize Your Return on Energy

Analyze your work based on the measure that I call "return on energy." Leaders in every field deliberately apply their talents and energies where they can achieve their greatest return on the amount of energy—mental, emotional, and physical—that they invest in any endeavor. They refuse to take on jobs or work in areas where they cannot perform at exceptional levels. They treat themselves as valuable resources and they spend their energies very carefully.

One of the questions that you might continually ask yourself is, "Is this the best possible use of my time and energy?"

Is what you are doing right now the most valuable thing that you could be doing, given your particular combination of talents and abilities? Often, answering this question will help you to see that there is a vast difference between what you are currently doing and what you should be doing if you want to be fulfilling more of your potential.

Do What You Love

Marsha Sinetar wrote a top-selling book a few years ago whose title says it all: *Do What You Love, the Money Will Follow* (Dell Publishing Company, 1987). Almost every really successful, happy man or woman will say that the reason for their success is that they are "doing what they love to do."

Whenever a person is unhappy for any reason, I always ask them how much they enjoy their work, and would they choose to do this type of work if there were other options open to them? Invariably when someone is generally unhappy with their life, especially a man, they are dissatisfied with their work for some reason.

Unfortunately, there is an old myth in our society that suggests that work is a penalty you pay during the day so that you can get your enjoyment from other things in the evenings and on the weekends. Many people view work as a punishment that is unavoidable. They try to do it as well as they need to so that they don't get fired, but they never really think about whether they enjoy it.

However, this attitude is not for you. Your life is too precious and valuable to spend it doing something you don't enjoy. Every minute of it should be spent doing things that you love and care about, and that make you happy.

The wonderful thing is that the highest paid people in America, and worldwide, are often working at jobs that they enjoy so much that they hate to go home at night, and the lowest paid people are invariably found at jobs they dislike, in which they are just going through the motions.

Two Questions to Test Job Suitability

Here are two simple tests to determine whether you are in the right job for you.

1. Would you continue to work at that job if you won a million dollars in the lottery tomorrow?

   If the first thing that you would do would be to quit your job if you had enough money, then this simply means that you are in the wrong position for you.

2. Use what I call the "clock test." People who are in the wrong job watch the clock all the time. They are very aware of what time they start, and what time they quit. People who

are in the right job are seldom aware of the clock, except to know how little time they have left to do the work they really enjoy.

However you measure it, choosing the right work for you is central to your enjoying high feelings of self-esteem and self-confidence, not only in your work, but in every other area of your life.

Commit to Excellence

Once you have chosen your ideal job or occupation for this stage of your career, your biggest responsibility is to make the decision to become very good, and then to become excellent, at what you do.

In a lengthy study on successful Americans, the Gallup organization discovered that "expertise," or being recognized by your peers as one of the very best in your field, was one of the essential ingredients for success in American life.

We said before that that self-confidence comes from positive *knowing*, rather than positive thinking. It is only when you know that you are outstanding in your chosen field that you really feel terrific about yourself, and that you enjoy high levels of self-confidence.

Men and women who are good at what they do, and who *know* that they are good at what they do, are very different from those who are only average. They walk and talk and dress and behave differently. They have an attitude of assurance and certainty about themselves that causes them to stand out in any group. They have a deep-down sense of self-worth and self-confidence that is evident to everyone around them.

Excellence Is Learnable

A man in his mid-20s came up to me at a seminar in Pittsburgh recently. He said that he had started in sales just over four years ago. When he began, he had no experience and knew nothing about either how to sell or his product and how it could benefit his prospects.

He told me that his basic sales training was provided to him by his manager in the form of my audio program, "The Psychology of Selling." As he listened to the program, which taught him how to sell professionally, step-by-step, he became excited about learning and about professional development. He listened to the audios, over and over, and then bought additional audio programs and began reading voraciously in the field of selling.

He told me that in his first year, in a very competitive market, he made $22,000. However, as he read and listened to audio programs, and attended seminars, he got better and better. In his second year he earned $48,000. He became totally committed to continuous learning, and in his third year he earned $94,000. In his fourth year, he earned just over $175,000, selling the same products, in the same competitive market, to the same customers, at the same prices and under the same economic conditions. And he had driven to the seminar in his new Mercedes.

Not everyone can experience such extraordinary financial results, but the most important thing about this young salesman was that he exuded self-confidence and personal pride from every pore. He had a positive self-image and high self-esteem. He was admired and respected by the people around him. And he was held up as a model to others of what they might become if they just worked on themselves and on their jobs hard enough.

The Law of Accumulation

This brings us to a very important mental principle called the "law of accumulation." The application of this law is a fundamental reason for success in every field, including yours. This law says that every great life or great career is an accumulation of hundreds, and perhaps thousands, of efforts that nobody ever sees or appreciates. Great success is the result of countless hours, maybe even months and years, of preparation and hard work toward the goal of becoming very good at what you are doing.

This law of accumulation says that life is very much like a balance sheet, with both credits and debits. Every time you do something positive to enhance your abilities and to improve your life, you get a credit on the credit side of your ledger. Each time you waste your time, or neglect to take advantage of an opportunity to learn and grow, you get a debit on the debit side of your ledger.

Here's the key: everything counts. Everything that you do or fail to do is written down and totaled up on your balance sheet. Everything that you do or fail to do, counts in some way. Nothing is neutral. Everything is either moving you toward a better life, or moving you away from it. Everything counts.

A successful, happy, self-confident person is an individual who has consciously and deliberately built up a lot of credits on his or her balance sheet. An unhappy, negative, or insecure person is a person who has a lot of debits on his or her balance sheet. Because the only things that count are your actions, it seems that every positive and constructive action you engage in adds up and increases your levels of self-confidence and self-esteem.

The Law of Incremental Improvement

Perhaps the most important corollary of the law of accumulation is what is called the law of incremental improvement. This is really the law that explains how you move from wherever you are to the top of your field. This is the law that explains all great success in America, or anywhere else in the world. This law simply states that a person becomes good at his or her chosen field by improving incrementally, continuously, over a long period of time.

My friend, Darren Hardy, has written a book entitled, *The Compound Effect* (Vanguard Press, 2011), in which he explains how it is that everything positive you do in your life compounds and multiplies, growing with force and power over the months and years. As Einstein said, "Compounding is the most powerful force in the universe."

Pattern Recognition

In a study on the subject of mastery, reported on in the magazine *Psychology Today*, the researchers concluded that mastery consisted of the ability to recognize a great variety of patterns in a given situation, based on what they called a "high level of integrative complexity."

Integrative complexity is defined as the ability to recognize patterns in a situation and to accurately predict what is likely to happen and the best action to take, based on previous experiences with similar situations.

For example, a sales person would achieve a high level of confidence and capability in a sales situation by having both studied his or her profession and by having been in countless previous sales situations. He or she would have developed the ability to integrate knowledge and experience and to recognize a particular pattern in the sales situation based on previous sales situations that were similar to this one.

An excellent business person is one who has developed this same capability of recognizing a pattern when it occurs again, drawing on previous experiences, and, therefore, responding effectively by doing and saying the right things to complete the business transaction successfully or making the correct investment decision.

The Grand Masters

The researchers found that a grand master in chess, for example, was able to recognize as many as 100,000 different patterns or layouts on the chess board and had developed a strategy to deal with each one. A national chess champion was able to recognize perhaps 50,000 patterns. A tournament chess player was able to recognize perhaps 10,000 patterns on the chessboard, and so on.

Their conclusion was that it takes several thousand hours of research and practice to achieve and perform at exceptional levels in any complex field or any difficult occupation or profession. Although there are prodigies, people who succeed in a short period of time, these are very rare.

Malcolm Gladwell, in his best-selling book, *Outliers* (Back Bay Books, 2011), quotes the extensive research that shows that it takes several years, on average, for a person to become excellent in his or her chosen field. According to Gladwell, mastery in any field requires 10,000 hours, or seven years of hard work, or both.

Most people only become wealthy after the age of 40 or 50, if they achieve it at all. It takes them many years of hard work, continuous learning, and experience to develop an extensive enough repertoire of patterns so they can recognize and take advantages of opportunities that appear to them. Up to that time, they make many mistakes: "two steps forward and one step back."

The Foundation of Self-Confidence

The law of incremental improvement is your key to an unlimited future of success, prosperity, and self-confidence. *It doesn't matter where you are starting from; all that matters is where you are going.* As Theodore Roosevelt said, "Do what you can, with what you have, where you are."

By applying the law of incremental improvement to yourself and your work, you can begin moving upward toward joining the great ones in your field. If you are doing what you love to do and you are doing it with all your heart, by engaging in continuous personal and professional improvement, you can begin to move forward at such a rapid rate that it will astonish you.

You've heard of the 80/20 rule, which says that 80 percent of the income goes to 20 percent of the people. Your goal, if you are not already there, should be to join the top 20 percent in your field. If you're in the top 20 percent, your job is to get into the top 10 percent, and then the top 5 percent, and then the top 4 percent, and so on.

Your goal should be to "be the best." Your goal is to be recognized by those around you as outstanding in your field. Your goal must be to pay any price, overcome any obstacle, and make any effort necessary to become excellent in your chosen career. In just a moment, I'll show you how.

Moving to the Top

There is one small problem that you need to deal with before you become one of the best in your field. Earlier in this book I said that most of us grow up with feelings of inferiority and inadequacy. Because of low self-esteem and selling ourselves short, many of us never even think about becoming excellent at our work. It never even occurs to us that we have the ability to learn anything we need to learn to be able to do an outstanding job at anything we put our minds to.

The fact is that, generally speaking, you have the capability to excel at anything that is really important to you. If anyone else has achieved a high level of competence in your field, then so can you. All you have to do is to do the same things, over and over, until sooner or later you get the same results that they have. This is the law of cause and effect in action. When you practice this law in conjunction with the law of incremental improvement, you can move from wherever you are to wherever you want to be.

Identify Your Key Skills

Just as choosing the right work or career for you requires self-analysis and self-awareness, moving to the top of your field requires that you take your existing position and break it down to what we call its key result areas (KRAs) or to its core competencies.

In every job, and in every company for that matter, there are a few key skills, seldom more than five to seven, that determine the success or failure of the person in that job.

Wherever an individual is having trouble in his or her career, it is usually because he or she is weak in one or more of these KRAs or core skills. Wherever a person is successful, it turns out that they are strong in all the key skills necessary for success in that job.

Here is a key discovery: Your weakest important skill determines the height of your success in your work.

You could be excellent at six out of seven of your key result areas, but your weakness in the seventh area can hold you back for years.

Analyze Your Skill Levels

Your first job is to break your work down into its component parts, its basic skills, and then honestly analyze your level of competence in each one, by giving yourself a grade on a scale from 1 to 10.

For example, if you are in sales, your KRAs or "core skills" might be prospecting, establishing rapport, identifying problems, presenting solutions, answering objection, closing the sale, and getting resales and referrals from satisfied customers. A weakness in any one of these areas could be fatal to your success and your income.

If you are in business, your KRAs could be leadership and management, strategic planning, marketing and sales, staffing and delegating, financial controls and administration, and production and quality controls. Each situation may be slightly different, but the same concept applies. Success begins by analyzing the individual parts of your performance and then making a plan to become very good in each area.

Deliberate Practice

One of the most important breakthroughs in personal performance and career success is described in Geoffrey Colvin's top-selling book, *Talent Is Overrated* (Portfolio Trade, 2010). Colvin shows that most people start their careers with limited marketable skills, and then develop from there.

It turns out that those executives who got to the top early in their careers developed the habit of identifying the most important skill they could develop at that stage of their career. They would then dedicate themselves to mastering that skill, one skill at a time.

Once they had developed a key skill, they would then identify the one skill that could help them to advance further. Their entire career ladder consisted of mastering each key skill, one at a time, until the "compound effect" took over, and they moved rapidly upward in their jobs.

Identify Your Key Skill

A good exercise is to ask yourself, "What is my limiting skill? What is it that I do, or don't do, that is determining the speed at which I succeed and move ahead in my job?"

What is the performance bottleneck or choke point in your work? What limits you or holds you back from getting to where you want to go? Sometimes, taking the time to develop one limiting skill will put your entire career onto the fast track.

A manager in one of my seminars asked me privately why it was that he was continually passed over for promotion at his engineering firm, even though his boss acknowledged that he did excellent work? I asked him about the qualities and activities of the highest paid engineers in the company.

It turned out that they (along with accountants, architects, and many other professionals) were "rainmakers." They had the ability to make presentations to clients, and to sell them on the idea of giving work to their firm.

He then told me that he was terrified of public speaking and any kind of selling. I told him that, if he wanted to move up in his firm, he should take a course in public speaking, overcome his fears, and begin bringing in business to his company.

A year later, I was giving another management seminar that he attended. He had taken my advice, joined Toastmasters, taken a Dale Carnegie course, and become a fluent and popular spokesman for his company. He had been promoted twice, his income was up 40 percent, and he was one of the most respected people in his firm. His whole life and career had been transformed by the development of a key skill.

All Skills Are Learnable

Once you have defined your ideal job, and then broken that job down into its constituent parts or core skills, and then made a plan to become very good in each part of your job, then your final key to self-motivation and a feeling of growth is to commit yourself to continuous, never-ending self-improvement. Make a decision right now to dedicate yourself to a lifetime process of personal and professional development.

Here are three simple rules that will change your life:

1. Invest 3 percent of your income back into yourself. Spend 3 percent of what you earn on personal research and development, on upgrading your skills and abilities, and on becoming better at performing the most important tasks that are required of you. If you invest 3 percent of your income back into yourself, you will never have to worry about money again.

2. Read for one hour or more each day in your chosen field, underlining and taking careful notes that you can review regularly.

    A simple technique is to read and underline with a red pen and then go back and transfer all of those key points into a spiral notebook. You can dictate the key points and have them typed up for you or you can use dictation software that translates your voice and which allows you to then print out the key points.

    You will then have a synopsis of the most important ideas in any book. When you review them, which only takes about 10 minutes or so, five or six times, you memorize almost all the key points. This method is used by some of the most successful men and women in America.

3. Listen to audio programs in your car. Turn your automobile into a *mobile classroom*, a university on wheels. Never drive your car without your educational audio programs playing.

According to the American Automobile Association, the average driver spends between five hundred and a thousand hours each year in their car. If you turn this driving time into "learning time," you can become one of the best educated people of your generation.

Your Most Valuable Financial Asset

Your ability to earn money by applying your knowledge and skill is the most important single source of money in your life. This is called your "earning power," and is the sum total of all your knowledge and skill applied to doing a job.

Your "earning ability" is your ability to get *results* that someone will pay you for. This capacity represents as much as 80 to 90 percent of your total net worth.

Your earning ability is either an appreciating asset, becoming more valuable each month and year, or a depreciating asset, losing value each month and year because of a failure to continually upgrade your skills.

One of the smartest expenditures you can make is to invest in your "earning ability," to become better at what pays you the most. This continuous investment in yourself will put you behind the wheel of your own life. It will assure you of greater success and self-confidence every day of your life, and by the law of indirect effort, a commitment to yourself will earn you the self-esteem, self-respect, and personal pride that you desire.

You will eventually achieve the competence and mastery in your field that generate the feelings of self-confidence that make you irresistible.

There is no limit to what you can accomplish if you know the direction in which you are going and you are willing to make the efforts to become excellent at what you do.

Action Exercises

1. Make a decision today to become excellent at what you do. Set it as a goal, make a plan, and work on it every day.

2. Identify the jobs or parts of your job that you most enjoy, and then seek a way to more and more of those jobs.

3. Identify those jobs in your career that have been easy to learn and which are easy to do, and look for ways to do more of them, more of the time.

4. Identify the KRAs of your work and give yourself a grade of 1–10 in each one. Remember that your weakest key skill sets the height of your success.

5. Identify the one skill that, if you were excellent at it consistently, would have the greatest positive impact on your career.

6. Develop a continuous learning plan for yourself, and dedicate yourself toward getting better and better at what you do.

7. Identify the most important result, or results, for which you are paid, and resolve to get more and better of those results each day.

CHAPTER 4

The Inner Game of Self-Confidence

Confidence doesn't come out of nowhere. It's a result of some-
thing . . . hours and days and weeks and years of constant work
and dedication.

—Roger Staubach

Aristotle wrote in his famous *Nichomachean Ethics* that the common aim of mankind is to be happy, however each person defines happiness. One thing we know is that the more confident and the better we feel about ourselves, the happier we are and the more effective we seem to be in everything we do.

Self-confidence, however, is really a state of mind based on your belief systems. Belief, or faith, enables you to act boldly in the face of uncertainty. Confidence enables you to face changes and difficulties and unexpected setbacks with calmness and clarity, and allows you to respond more effectively under any circumstances.

The Law of Belief

The law of belief, an important corollary of the law of cause and effect, says that "your beliefs become your realities." You do not believe what you see, but you *see* what you believe. William James of Harvard said that "Belief creates the actual fact."

In the Bible, it says, "According to your belief, it is done unto you." If you believe strongly enough and confidently enough, your outer world will tend to conform to a pattern consistent with these beliefs.

In fact, your world today is largely an out-picturing of your innermost beliefs and convictions. You behave on the outside based on your beliefs on the inside. You see the world around you based on your beliefs about reality, regardless of whether they are correct.

How can you determine you true beliefs? Simple. You can tell what you really believe by observing what you do and what you don't do. You can tell what you believe by listening to your opinions, your conversations, and by noting your decisions. When you truly believe yourself to be an exceptional human being, possessed of remarkable capabilities, you will walk and talk and act that way, and your inner convictions will become your outer realities. As the Bible says, "All things are possible to him that believeth."

The Power of Belief

There is a story about a man, many years ago, whose business was in serious trouble. He had lost some big sales, he was deeply in debt, and his suppliers and creditors were closing in on him.

He didn't know whether he should continue struggling or just declare bankruptcy and let his business fold. He decided to go for a walk in the park that evening to think it over and decide what to do.

He was standing in the park on a small bridge looking down at the water, when an older man appeared out of the darkness. Seeing his downcast look, the older man stopped and demanded to know what the matter was.

For some reason, the businessman told him about all his financial problems and how close his business was to collapsing, even though it was a good business and had a good potential future. The older man listened intently, and then said, "I think I can help you."

He pulled a checkbook out of his pocket, asked the man his name, and wrote out a check for him, pushed it into his hand, and said, "Take this money. Meet me here exactly one year from today and you can pay me back at that time." Then, the older man turned and disappeared into the darkness.

The $500,000 Check

When the businessman returned to his office, he opened up the check and found that it was for $500,000. He thought it was just a joke until he read the signature. The signature read, "John D. Rockefeller." He had received a check for half a million dollars from the richest man in the world, at that time, the man who had formed the Standard Oil Company and who was well known for giving money away to others.

At first, he thought he would cash the check and solve all his financial problems. But then he decided that instead, he would put the check in his safe, knowing that he could draw upon it any time. He would use this knowledge of having this amount of money to deal more confidently with his suppliers and creditors, and to turn his business around.

With renewed enthusiasm, he plunged back into his business and made deals, negotiated settlements, extended terms of payment, and closed several large sales. Within a few months, his business was back on top, out of debt, and making money.

The Man on the Bridge

One year later, he went back to the bridge in the park with the uncashed check still in his hand. He could hardly wait to tell the older man what had happened. At exactly the agreed time, the older man emerged from the darkness once more. Just as the businessman was about to give him back his check and tell him his exciting story of success and achievement over the previous 12 months, a nurse came running out of the darkness up to the old man and grabbed his arm.

She apologized to the businessman, saying, "I'm so glad I caught him. I hope he hasn't been bothering you. He's always escaping from the rest home and going around telling people that he is John D. Rockefeller." She took the old man's arm and led him away.

The businessman just stood there, stunned. All year long he had been wheeling and dealing, buying and selling, and building his business with the calm, confident knowledge that he had a $500,000 check in his safe that he could cash at any time.

It suddenly dawned on him that he had made his business successful based on his beliefs, even though the information on which his beliefs were based was false. It had been his self-confidence in action that was responsible for the turnaround in his affairs.

First Convince Yourself

Your job is to achieve the same level of confidence and belief as that possessed by that businessman. The world will largely accept you at your own estimation. It is yourself that you have to convince, before you can convince anyone else. But once you are absolutely sure that you have what it takes to master any situation, you will act in such a way that your beliefs will become your reality.

We are really talking here about what we call mental fitness or the hardy, resilient personality. Mental fitness is subject to the law of cause and effect. You can develop the kind of unshakable self-confidence that you desire by simply repeating certain thoughts and actions over and over, until they are driven deep into your subconscious mind and take on a power of their own. You can build your level of mental fitness just as you would build your level of physical fitness by working on your "mental muscles" in a specific way until they are as strong and effective as you want.

The Power of Suggestion

Perhaps the most powerful influence in determining your mental and emotional state at any time is the *power of suggestion*. The power of suggestion begins influencing you even before you are born, and continues from infancy and throughout your life, making you the kind of person you are today.

Experts say that fully 95 percent of what you do, say, think, and feel is determined by environmental and psychological suggestive influences around you. For example, the average person is so susceptible to suggestive influences, that a rude word from another person may cause him or her to be upset and angry for hours. On the other hand, a kind word of praise or recognition may cause him or her to be positive and happy for the rest of the day. We are all very susceptible to the suggestive influences that surround us.

Control Your Suggestive Environment

To enjoy high levels of self-confidence, you must be able to make up your own mind and free yourself from any influences that cause you to feel negative or unhappy for any reason. You must take full control over your own thinking and over your own suggestive environment, making sure that what you are allowing into your mind is consistent with the things you want and the person you want to be. And you must work to keep out all other influences.

There are three forms of suggestion that can determine how you feel about yourself and how you think. The first is called external suggestion. These are all the activities that go on around you, from the moment you get up in the morning until your last communication or information input in the evening.

Depending on how open and receptive you are, you can be inordinately influenced by television, radio, newspaper, the Internet, conversations, work experiences, feedback from superiors, interactions with members of your family, even problems in traffic or changes of temperature on the outside.

The great majority of people allow much of their lives to be determined by what is going on around them; they convince themselves that they are thinking independently, whereas they are merely reacting to whatever happens instead.

Control Your Emotions

This is why the negative emotions that upset and disturb you are usually unconscious, unthinking reactions that are triggered by external events. We know this is true because no one would consciously and deliberately decide to feel negative, angry, or upset. When people are in control of their emotions, they choose to feel happy.

For example, one of the most common expressions of negative emotions has to do with what are called conditioned responses. These are automatic responses that we engage in when somebody pushes one of our hot buttons. A hot button is a habitual negative way of reacting to an experience or to something that someone says. Each person has a series of these buttons, and when we know a person well, especially in an intimate relationship, we know just what buttons to push to get whatever reactions we want.

When one of your buttons is pushed, such as when someone mentions someone or something that you feel very strongly about, you respond with anger and defensiveness. If you hate to get cut off in traffic and somebody cuts you off inadvertently, your hot button will be triggered and you will be talking angrily to yourself and to anyone else who will listen for the foreseeable future.

Think Before You React

One of the ways to take control of your mind is to identify, in advance, the various external factors that cause you to become angry or upset. Make a list of everything that happens that might cause you have a tendency to respond negatively. Then, consciously make the decision that, in the future, when one of these issues comes up, you will instead respond calmly and positively and not allow yourself to become upset and angry.

Each time something happens that would normally trigger a negative response from you, consciously decide not to respond or not to react in any way. Smile, take a deep breath and remain calm. The more you practice this, the easier it will become. You will become more positive and optimistic. Your self-confidence will go up and you will feel more in charge of your own life. You will begin to free yourself from being a slave to external suggestions that control your mental state.

The Power of Self-Suggestion

The second form of suggestion is called "self-suggestion." "Self-suggestion" is when you put both hands on the controls of your own mental life, or step up to the keyboard of your own mental computer, and consciously program your subconscious mind with the thoughts and feelings that you desire. Self-suggestion is your key to building the kind of belief system deep within yourself that leads to unshakable self-confidence. The reason that self-suggestion works so well is because of the law of substitution.

The law of substitution says that your conscious mind can only hold one thought at a time; positive or negative. If you consciously choose to hold a positive word or picture in your mind, you simultaneously block out the various inputs from external sources that might cause your thinking and feeling to be negative or inconsistent with your true desires.

For example, if, whenever you begin to feel tense or uneasy or angry about something, you switch your mind and start thinking about your goals, your mind will switch from negative to positive instantly, and you will feel good about yourself again. The thought of a goal, which is positive and future-oriented, is inherently uplifting. You cannot think about your goal and be upset or angry at the same time. By using the law of substitution, you take full control over your suggestive environment, and over the information that reaches your subconscious mind.

Make Self-Control into a Game

When something negative or unexpected happens to you, immediately seize the moment as an opportunity to demonstrate calmness and self-control. Make it a game. Instead of allowing yourself to feel negative, deliberately force yourself to substitute something positive.

Here is an affirmation that has been very helpful to me. I repeat it over and over until it becomes automatic, in almost every situation. When something goes wrong, I immediately catch myself by saying, "Every situation is a positive situation if viewed as an opportunity for growth and self-mastery."

Whatever it is, I take a deep breath, relax, smile, and say, "Every situation is a positive situation if viewed as an opportunity for growth and self-mastery." I then look within the situation for something that I can learn that will help me to grow and develop greater self-mastery.

This is a simple "mind game" that enables me to stay relaxed and in control of my emotions. It will work for you, as well. Just give it a try.

The Power of Autosuggestion

Autosuggestion takes place when you have repeated messages to your subconscious mind so often that they take on a power of their own. They function automatically. We have found continually that happy, optimistic people have programmed themselves to respond in a happy and optimistic way to almost every situation. You can do the same thing.

All of life is bound up and determined by your responses. It is not what happens to you, but how you react to what happens to you that counts. It is not the cards that you are dealt, but the way you play the cards that determines how well you do in the game of life. Your job is to consciously decide to use your willpower to keep your mind clear and to keep yourself positive and functioning at your best.

A Quick Review

In Chapter 1, we talked about how important it is for your self-confidence for you to have clear values and to organize your life so that it is consistent with those values.

In Chapter 2, we talked about the importance of having goals for every part of your life and assuring that your goals and your values are congruent.

In Chapter 3, we talked about how important it is for you to commit yourself to achieving mastery in your chosen field, consistent with your goals and values.

In this chapter, you will learn a series of mental-fitness techniques that you can use to program your subconscious mind. You will learn how to develop the absolute conviction and confidence that you can achieve anything you set your mind to, and you will learn how to make this self-confident response an automatic reaction to anything that happens.

Take Charge of Your Life

The starting point of taking full control over your conscious and your subconscious mind is for you to accept complete responsibility for everything that you think, say, and do. You are responsible for whatever happens to you, and especially you are responsible for your responses to the inevitable ups and downs of daily life. As Eleanor Roosevelt said, "No one can make you feel inferior without your consent."

I used to think that setting goals and making plans was the starting point of success in life. After a while, I changed my mind because I realized that something else actually comes first. What comes first is the acceptance of complete responsibility for yourself and for everything that happens to you.

Real maturity begins when you finally realize that no-one is coming to the rescue. It is only when you accept total responsibility for your life situation, with no excuses and no blaming of others, that you move into a mental position to kick the long ball in your own life. It is only when you have accepted 100 percent responsibility for yourself that you are ready to take the next step and decide exactly what it is you want and exactly what it is you want to do.

Accepting responsibility is not an option that is open to the individual. It is mandatory. It is an absolute fact of human existence. You do not have the luxury of blaming others or making excuses for parts of your life that are not satisfactory.

As Henry Ford II said, "Never complain, never explain." No one *makes you* do anything or feel anything. You are where you are and what you are because you have decided to be there. Everything that you are or ever will be is entirely up to you. If there is any effect in your life that you're not happy about, it is solely up to you to change the causes. You are completely responsible.

Actions Have Consequences

Fully mature people accept that their actions have consequences. A fully functioning adult knows that he or she can choose an action, but once the action is taken, both predictable and unpredictable consequences will follow. The true adult accepts that for every cause, there will be an effect. For every action, there will be a reaction.

You can choose the action, before you act, but you cannot choose or control the consequence or reaction afterward. Intelligent adults are very careful about the thoughts they think and the actions that they take. They do not fool themselves or engage in self-delusion. They don't pretend that things might happen differently, nor do they trust to luck.

Inactions also have consequences. What are called "crimes of omission" are often more serious to your long-term prospects than the mistakes you make. Omitting to think through your values, set clear goals, make plans, commit to excellence, and so on, can be disastrous to your possibilities of great success.

Problems versus Facts

The starting point of success is the acceptance of reality. "What cannot be cured must be endured." Often people will come to me with challenges they are facing, and I will ask them this simple question. "Is this a problem or is this a fact?"

If it's a problem, it's amenable to a solution. There is something that you can do to change it. If you are not happy with the situation, it is up to you to go and do whatever you can to resolve it.

A fact, however, is different from a problem. It is something that exists, like the weather, like rain or snow. There is nothing that you can do about it. You can solve problems, but the reality principle says that you have to learn to live with facts.

Something unfortunate that has happened is a fact. A sale that did not go through, a business deal that collapsed, a relationship that didn't work out—all of these are facts. Many people waste an enormous amount of emotional energy struggling with facts when they would be much better off concentrating on doing better in the future.

Accepting Responsibility Is the Beginning

Your goal is to be happy, confident, and optimistic. The way that you achieve this is by making these positive responses so automatic that you remain predominantly happy, confident, and optimistic, no matter what happens.

You can achieve this result by taking specific, proven, practical steps, that have been used by millions of people and which work with virtually unfailing certainty. The starting point is accepting complete responsibility for every aspect of your life.

Control Your Thoughts

You demonstrate this attitude of responsibility by exerting your freedom to choose the thoughts you wish to hold in your conscious mind. You choose to think positive, constructive thoughts rather than negative, destructive thoughts.

Psychologists refer to this as the cognitive-control method. Cognitive control simply means that you control your thoughts, keep them positive, and repeat positive messages to yourself over and over until they become automatic responses to daily life.

Positive Self-Talk

The first mental-fitness technique is that of positive self-talk or the use of *positive affirmations*. The way you talk to yourself has an inordinate impact on your thinking and feeling. Many researchers, including Dr. Martin Seligman of the University of Pennsylvania, have discovered that high-performing men and women talk to themselves differently from low-performing men and women.

Basically, your self-talk, or your inner dialogue, determines the tone of your emotional life. You are happy or sad, positive or negative, depending on what you say to yourself and how you interpret events to yourself as you go along.

For example, if you are cut off in traffic and you immediately become angry and begin thinking about how stupid and irresponsible and what a bad driver the other person is, you will trigger a very different reaction than if, when you are cut off in traffic, you excuse the other person by thinking to yourself that he or she must be late, distracted, or must not have seen you. It may be exactly the same external event, but the way you interpret it and your ensuing conversation with yourself will determine whether you experience positive or negative emotions about the situation.

Your Interpretive Style

The starting point of using positive self-talk is to interpret everything that happens to you in a favorable way. Become what W. Clement Stone called an "inverse paranoid." Imagine that the whole world is in a giant conspiracy to help you to be successful and happy. Imagine that everything that happens is happening to teach you something valuable and to move you closer to achieving your most important goals. Just as a paranoid is convinced that there is a conspiracy against him, an *inverse* paranoid is convinced that there is a conspiracy for him or her.

Practice the wonderful mental quality of *serendipity*. In the fairy tale, the three princes of Serendip traveled around finding that every apparently negative or calamitous event they witnessed turned out to be positive and beneficial in the end. Make it a game to look for the good in every situation.

Practice Positive Expectations

The law of expectations says that *whatever you expect, with confidence, becomes your own self-fulfilling prophecy*. When you develop an attitude of positive self-expectancy, you become a more optimistic and cheerful person. Whatever happens, you immediately interpret it in the best way possible.

In Napoleon Hill's famous book, *Think and Grow Rich* (Tribeca Books, 2010), he wrote that one of the characteristics of the most successful men and women in America is that they always look for the opportunity or benefit within every setback or obstacle. Because of the law of substitution, if you are looking into every difficult situation for the lesson you can learn or for the possible opportunity it might contain, your mind will remain positive and you will continue to function at your best.

Talk to Yourself Positively

Whenever you think of an upcoming event, talk to yourself in positive language. Perhaps the most powerful affirmation of all for building self-confidence is for you to repeat, over and over, 50–100 times per day, the words, "I can do it! I can do it! I can do it!"

These simple words are the verbal antidote to the fear of failure, which, as you know, is the great destroyer of self-confidence and probably the primary reason for failure in adult life. However, you can diminish the fear of failure in any situation by repeating, "I can do it! I can do it! I can do it!"

Whenever you think of an event that causes you to feel nervous or insecure, whenever you have something coming up that fills you with trepidation, exert your powers of self-talk and self-suggestion by saying, "I can do it!" to cancel out and override any negative emotions associated with it.

Control Your Thoughts and Feelings

The most powerful affirmation for building self-esteem are the words, "I like myself! I like myself! I like myself!"

These simple words, repeated often enough, with energy and enthusiasm, will eventually be accepted by your subconscious mind. As your subconscious mind accepts this message of self-liking, your self-esteem goes up and your ability to perform and your levels of effectiveness improve in every area of your life.

If you want to do your work better, just say, "I love my job! I love my job! I love my job!"

In their best-selling book, *Success Through a Positive Mental Attitude* (Pocket Books, 2007), W. Clement Stone and Napoleon Hill recommend that you repeat, several times a day, the words, "I feel happy! I feel healthy! I feel terrific!"

One of my favorite affirmations, whenever I'm worried about anything, is to cancel it by saying, "I believe in the perfect outcome of every situation in my life. I believe in the perfect outcome of every situation in my life."

You will find that it is almost impossible to worry and fret about anything while you are repeating this kind of positive message to yourself.

Unlimited Potential

Your potential is unlimited using affirmations. Remember that affirmations are a way of programming your subconscious mind. By repeated affirmations, you can instill within your mind powerful, positive commands that will eventually determine your automatic thoughts, feelings, and responses.

In order for affirmations to work, they must be phrased using the three Ps. They must be in the present tense, positive, and personal.

The affirmations, "I can do it! I like myself! I feel terrific!" are all positive, present tense, and personal. The subconscious is very *literal* in nature and can only accept commands phrased in the present tense. For some reason, it ignores negative commands and focuses only on the positive message.

If a person says, "I will not smoke again," the subconscious mind drops out the "will" and "not" and only accepts the message, "I smoke again. I smoke again." It is better to say, "I am a non-smoker." The subconscious can form a clear picture of a nonsmoker and will eventually adjust a person's habits and tastes to the point where they stop smoking altogether.

You can create affirmations for each of your goals, and by repeating them continually, you program them deeper into your subconscious mind until they take on a power of their own. You then find yourself automatically motivated to do the things necessary to achieve them.

Written Affirmations

The second technique you can use to keep your mind positive and to achieve your goals faster, is to write out your goals in the form of affirmations on 3 × 5 index cards. Write them in large black letters, and then read and reread the cards several times each day, reciting the affirmation to yourself each time.

This and every other method or technique that you use to convince yourself that your goal is achievable will also help to build your self-esteem and self-confidence. This attitude or belief will cause you to take the specific actions that will eventually make your goals a reality.

Practice Visualization

The third technique for building self-confidence is the use of positive visualization. This is the process of creating clear mental pictures of the person that you want to be, doing the things you want to do, and achieving the goals you want to achieve. Because your subconscious mind cannot tell the difference between a real experience and one that you vividly imagine, it will give you the thoughts and feelings that would accompany your realization of your mental pictures.

What determines the impact of visualization is the amount of emotion that you combine with the picture when you hold it in your conscious mind for reception by your subconscious. The more emotion with which you visualize, the faster the visualization will emerge in your reality.

Mental Rehearsal

An effective way of visualizing is a peak performance technique called "mental rehearsal." In mental rehearsal, you go through an upcoming event in your mind, detail by detail, and imagine it happening perfectly, with you being completely successful in the end.

Prior to any event of importance, you recall and relive a previous experience where you performed well. You take a few moments to replay in your mind a picture of the last time you did this particular activity successfully.

If you have to write an exam of any kind, take a few moments to close your eyes, breathe deeply, and see yourself writing the exam easily, knowing all the answers. If you have to make a sales call, take a few moments prior to the sales call, close your eyes and see yourself in the sales call, perfectly relaxed, positive, calm, and in complete control.

See the prospect or customer responding positively toward you and signing the contract or check at the end of your visit. If you have an interview coming up, take a few moments to rehearse the interview in your mind. Go through every stage of it, see yourself performing at your very best, and visualize the other person responding to you in a positive and productive way.

Improve Your Mental Pictures

All improvement in your life begins with an improvement in your mental pictures. If you want to wear beautiful clothes, you should purchase and read magazines filled with pictures of models wearing the kind of clothes you desire. Visit clothing stores of the very best quality and try on clothes that you eventually want to own. Flood your mind with pictures and sensations of the reality that you desire to experience.

If you want to drive a better car, go and test-drive exactly the automobile that you desire. Get the brochure on the car and put pictures of the car all over your house or apartment.

A friend of mine used this exact technique to get his dream car. He cut out a picture of the new BMW he wanted and put it on the steering wheel of his car. Each time he looked down, he imagined he was already driving his dream car. Within one year he had it.

When you take your desired car for a test drive, fill your senses with every detail of the automobile. Touch it and smell it and look at the upholstery and the dashboard and the interior design. Your main job is to get a clear picture for your subconscious to go to work on.

Get Your Dream House

If you wish to live in a nicer home, go out to open houses in the neighborhood that you desire to live in. Walk through the homes and imagine living there. Don't worry for the moment whether it is possible or how high the prices are. Your primary job is simply to "get the picture." Get magazines filled with pictures of beautiful homes and read them from cover to cover. Practice the law of concentration by allowing your mind to dwell on the things you want over and over.

Especially, get the feeling. The key to activating your mental powers through affirmation and visualization is for you to also imagine exactly how you would feel if you had already achieved your goal. Imagine the feelings of pride and happiness and self-esteem that you would enjoy as a result of obtaining your objectives. This emotional component is the catalyst that causes the other mental programming techniques to work more rapidly.

The End of the Movie

One of the best methods for programming your mind and building your beliefs is what is called the end-of-the-movie exercise. This is a tremendous tool for building self-confidence prior to any upcoming situation. It is very simple.

Imagine that you have gone to a movie only to find that there are 10 minutes left of the movie before it begins again. Instead of waiting in the lobby, you decide to go into the theater and watch the last 10 minutes. You see how the plot works itself out, how the drama is resolved and how the movie ends satisfactorily. You then wait for a few minutes and when the movie starts again, you watch the movie from the beginning.

Only now, however, you know that it turns out all right. You know how each part of the plot eventually resolves itself satisfactorily. Instead of becoming caught up in the drama and uncertainty and tension, you simply relax, peacefully, knowing how it all turns out at the end of the movie.

You can apply this same technique to almost everything you do. You can manufacture your own self-confidence by imagining that no matter what your situation, everything turns out perfectly in the end. Create that "end of the movie" feeling in yourself whenever you think of an upcoming event or problem that causes you any tension or insecurity at all. Prior to a meeting or a sales call or an interview, take a few moments to get that "end of the movie" feeling. Then, just relax. No matter what happens in the interim, you don't have to worry at all. You already know that the situation resolves itself with good for all concerned.

The interesting thing is that if you do this repeatedly, not only will you experience higher levels of self-confidence, but events in your life will have a tendency to turn out as well or better than you could have asked for or expected.

Feed Your Mind

The fourth mental fitness technique, and another way to build your self-confidence, is to continually feed your mind with books, magazines, and audio programs containing positive and uplifting messages.

Just as you become what you eat, you do become what you think about, as well. Everything that you take into your conscious mind, positive or negative, is either raising or lowering your self-esteem or self-confidence. To practice "cognitive control," you must be consciously aware of the suggestive influences around you and make every effort to assure that they are positive and consistent with your goals and desires.

Get Around Positive People

One of the most powerful suggestive influences in your life, perhaps the single influence that decides your success or failure more than any other controllable factor, is the kind of people that you associate with on a regular basis.

The fifth technique to keep yourself confident and optimistic is to be around positive people, and get away from negative people. Fly with the eagles, rather than scratching with the turkeys. Resolve today to get the negative people out of your life.

Because you are so inordinately influenced by other people—the people you work with and socialize with and spend time with—you must do everything to assure that you are surrounded by the kind of people you like, enjoy, and who make you feel good.

Research has shown that habitual association with critical, complaining people can be enough by itself to sabotage all your chances for success and happiness. Negative people drag you down. They rob you of energy and enthusiasm.

Attract Positive People into Your Life

Fortunately, the law of attraction works very quickly when applied to people. You can begin to change your human environment by beginning, first of all, to think about the kind of people that you admire and want to be like. Think about the men and women, living or dead, whose qualities you respect and whose lives you would like to emulate.

Read stories and biographies of successful men and women. Read magazine articles and interviews with people who are going somewhere with their lives. Begin associating with winners by first identifying with them *mentally*. As you think about people you admire, you will experience a subtle change in your thought patterns. As a result, you will begin to attract positive people into your life.

At the same time, you will activate the law of repulsion, and negative people will start to move away from you. Just as positive, goal-oriented people will start to find you interesting, as you become a more positive person, negative people will tend to find you unenjoyable and uninteresting. In no time at all, your human environment will begin to change for the better.

Everything Counts

By the way, if all these exercises in mental programming seem like a lot of work, remember that both actions and inactions have *consequences*. Like the law of sowing and reaping, whatever you sow, or fail to sow, is going to determine what you reap in the end.

The law of accumulation reminds us that everything counts. Every positive step you take is moving you toward building a great life for yourself. Every positive word or thought or image is deepening your belief and increasing your confidence in your ability to achieve wonderful things.

Finally, remember the law of reversibility. If you act in a manner consistent with high performance and high self-confidence, those very actions will generate the feelings consistent with them. Every positive, constructive action that you take in the direction of your dreams and goals will reinforce your belief in yourself and in your ability to accomplish your ideals.

Take Action Continually

Keep your vision clearly before you and take continuous positive action, every hour and every day. Develop a sense of urgency. Move quickly when opportunity presents itself. Maintain a bias for action.

Fast tempo is essential to success. And the faster you move, the better you will feel. The faster you move, the more energy you will have. And the faster you move, the higher will be your self-esteem and self-confidence.

The world can really be divided into two categories, the talkers and the doers. The world is full of talkers who seem to be convinced that if they talk about it enough it is the same as actually doing it.

But you are a *doer*, and it is always the doers who have been the movers and shakers throughout human history. It is the men and women who think, plan, and then take consistent, persistent action, who make things happen. When you engage in continuous action, not only will you feel terrific about yourself, but your ability to do whatever you want to do will grow by leaps and bounds. You will eventually become unstoppable!

Action Exercises

1. Create a clear, exciting mental picture of your most important goal as if it already existed, in every detail.

2. Each day, act as if you were already the positive, self-confident, successful person that you are going to be.

3. Practice "mental rehearsal" prior to every event of importance. Close your eyes, take a deep breath, create a mental picture of complete success, and get the feeling of calmness and confidence you desire.

4. Resolve today to accept complete responsibility for your life, for everything you are today, and for everything that you will ever be in the future.

5. Write your main goals on 3 × 5-inch cards and review them twice each day until they are programmed deeply into your subconscious mind.

6. Make a decision to associate only with positive people, and get the negative people out of your life.

7. Feed your mind daily with a steady stream of positive books, audios, conversations, and other suggestive influences that are consistent with the best person you could possibly be.

CHAPTER 5

Capitalizing on Your Strengths

I have learned that success is to be measured not so much by the position one has reached in life as by the obstacles he has overcome while trying to succeed.

—Booker T. Washington

elf-confidence goes hand-in-hand with winning, with self-esteem, with success and happiness in everything you do. The more self-confidence you have, the more things you will try, and, by the law of averages, the more things you are likely to achieve.

The more self-confidence you have, the less you will be affected by temporary setbacks and disappointments. The more self-confidence you have, the more likely it is that you will have a long, exciting life, full of riches, rewards, and self-satisfaction. Achieving these goals is the whole aim of this book.

One of the starting points of self-confidence is for you to recognize that you have tremendous strengths of ability and character that you can bring to bear to accomplish almost anything you want.

You are extraordinary! The odds are more than 50 billion to 1 against there ever being anyone with the unique combination of talents, skills, and abilities that you bring to your life and to your world. The incredible things that you can do and be, no one knows, not even you. However, the one thing we do know is that virtually everything noteworthy that you will ever achieve will come from your ability to identify your areas of greatest strength and then to capitalize on them in every situation.

Your Area of Excellence

Each person has one or more "areas of excellence" that, if properly exploited, would enable them to be, have, and do, almost anything they could possibly want. Each person, as the result of years of education and experience, has developed possibilities that make him or her different from all other people. The men and women who achieve the most, in every field, are invariably those who have taken the time to identify their areas of greatest strengths and then to capitalize on them continuously.

We said earlier that life is the study of attention. Where your attention goes, there will your heart be, too. The people, things, and events that hold your attention are indicative of your entire mental makeup. The things you are interested in are an indication of what you should be doing more of.

Choose the Right Field

In one longitudinal study examining 1,500 men and women who started out eager and ambitious at the beginning of their careers, they found that only 83 of them, over the course of 20 years, became millionaires.

When they went back and studied the attitudes and decisions of these people, as they had evolved over the 20 years, they found that all millionaires had one thing in common. They had all chosen fields they enjoyed and then become totally absorbed in what they were doing.

They had gone to work in an area of endeavor in which they were extremely interested and which held their entire attention. They had then thrown their whole hearts into becoming very good in that area, developing the strengths necessary to succeed in that field. They had then capitalized on those strengths by becoming better and better progressively over time.

The conclusion of the study was that success, wealth, and happiness seemed to occur when a person was completely pre-occupied doing something else. The wealthy people in this study never set out to make a lot of money. Instead, they set out to find fields that they really enjoyed, and then they devoted themselves to them. The money came as an afterthought.

Happiness and Satisfaction

The flip side of this equation is that you will never really be happy or satisfied until you have found a way to apply your unique human capabilities to your life and to your career. In the book, *Working*, by Studs Terkel (Pantheon Books, 1974), he reports that more than 80 percent of Americans do not feel that their full potential is being utilized in their work. They may be busy and they may be reasonably satisfied, but, way down deep, they feel that there is far more that they could do if given the right situation and the right opportunity. You probably feel this way yourself, from time to time.

This is called the feeling of divine discontent. It is a feeling of uneasiness and dissatisfaction that arises whenever you are not fully challenged by what you are doing. To enjoy high levels of self-confidence and self-esteem, you must be working at the outer edge of your envelope. You must be stretching your capabilities continually. You must have a feeling that you are growing, day by day, with the challenges that your work is putting on you.

Without that feeling of challenge and growth, you will experience a nagging discontent, and this is a good sign. Discontent and dissatisfaction almost always precede a constructive change that forces you to change and starts you growing, once more.

Living Congruently

In Chapter 1, we spoke about how important values are to your self-confidence. Men and women with clear values, who are living their lives consistent with their highest aspirations, are those who have a deep sense of self-confidence and well-being. We also said that the most important value you can have is the value of integrity. Integrity is the value that guarantees all the others. Having integrity means that you will not compromise on what you believe to be right, in any area.

Integrity is absolutely essential if you want to capitalize on your strengths. It means, more than anything, looking at yourself honestly and making your decisions based on the fact that you are an extraordinary human being. Your feelings are very valuable clues to your choices and behavior. Your peace of mind and personal satisfaction is perhaps the most accurate guide you will ever have to doing what is right for you.

Courage Is Essential

In combination with integrity, courage is the most important quality you can have if you want to be happy and self-confident. If integrity means being honest with yourself, then courage means having the strength of mind to follow where your heart leads you. Courage means having the ability to push aside all other considerations in order to remain true to the very best that is in you.

Winston Churchill said, "Courage is rightly considered the foremost of the virtues, for upon it, all others depend."

You know by now that fear is the greatest single enemy of self-confidence and self-fulfillment. It is not that people don't know what to do; it is usually that they are afraid to do what their hearts tell them to do. However, when you build up your courage, act by act, you gradually overcome your fears. With courage, your whole world opens up before you. Your self-confidence increases. You reach the point at which there are no longer any limitations on what you will attempt and what you will commit yourself to.

Follow Your Heart

One of the greatest of the impressionist painters was a man named Paul Gauguin. He lived in Paris, had a family, and worked in the post office for many years. In the evenings, he visited the cafes frequented by the impressionist painters of Paris, getting to know them and asking them questions. He was fascinated by painting. The whole idea of painting absorbed all his attention. It was all he thought about. And yet with a family and a full-time job, there was no way he could devote himself to the painting he wanted so badly to do.

One day, in a move that shocked everybody, he gave up his job as a postal inspector, left his family, and moved to the South Sea island of Tahiti. There, he began painting, poor quality at the beginning, but gradually improving as he developed his skill.

His paintings now are worth hundreds of thousands, even millions, of dollars, and they hang in the finest museums in the world.

He is considered by many to be one of the most important paint-ers of the last three hundred years. In a way, he was like Grandma Moses in that he finally decided to follow his heart and concentrate on what he had been interested in for all those years.

Be Honest with Yourself

To follow your heart, you don't necessarily need to make dramatic changes in your life or in your relationships. What you do need to do is to see yourself *honestly*, as you really are, and have the courage to channel your energies and focus your strengths into your areas of greatest potential. When you do this, you will soon realize that you have made one of the best decisions of your life.

Each person has great strengths and potentialities, and each person is put on this earth to harness those strengths and apply them to benefiting themselves and mankind. The life stories of the great men and women of history are usually stories of people who discovered their strengths and utilized them to the fullest degree.

Churchill was a great statesman and orator. Florence Nightingale was a tremendous organizer. Florence Chadwick was an incredibly strong swimmer. Abraham Lincoln was a far-sighted and compas-sionate politician and president. Mother Theresa was a truly loving human being with an infinite capacity to care for and support the sick and dying people of Calcutta. Joe Montana was a quarterback with an incredible throwing arm with the Washington Redskins.

All around you, you see men and women who have grabbed their major talents, like catching a pass in a football game, and are running for the goalposts. You can do the same if you have the courage to follow your heart.

Compensating for Weaknesses

No discussion of strengths would be complete without a discussion of *weaknesses*. Strong people have strong weaknesses, as well. In fact, most people have far more weaknesses than they have strengths. You may be strong in a few areas, but weak in hundreds of other areas.

Weaknesses are an inevitable and unavoidable fact of life. As Peter Drucker said, "All innovations must be simple if they are to work, because there are only incompetent people to carry them out. The one thing that we will always have in abundance is incompetence."

Drucker wasn't being unkind. He was being realistic and pointing out that *most* people are incompetent, or at best average, just in different areas. The challenge with human weaknesses is that unhappy and unsuccessful people have a tendency to focus on them. They become preoccupied with their weaknesses and think about their lack of talent and ability too much of the time. They lose sight of the fact that each person has strengths that may need to be developed, and that these strengths can bring them everything they want. Instead, they dwell continually on their areas of lesser competence rather than on their areas of potential excellence.

Developing Strength and Resiliency

We are all brought up with feelings of inferiority and inadequacy. Our self-esteem and self-confidence are fragile. Our positive feelings about ourselves are like balloons—easily popped. We have to work on ourselves for a long time to build ourselves up to the point at which we are tough and resilient, especially in the areas in which we make mistakes and drop the ball.

Every person is a combination of peaks and valleys. You have areas of great potential strength and you have multiple areas of weakness, where you perform in an average or mediocre way. Drucker also wrote: "The goal of business is to maximize strengths and make weaknesses irrelevant."

The law of concentration has an inordinate impact on the person you become. Whatever you dwell on grows in your life. Strong, competent people are those who dwell on their strengths and abilities. Weak people are those who dwell on their weaknesses and their inabilities.

You always have the choice of looking at your glass as being either half full or half empty. However, to develop and maintain high levels of self-confidence and the success and happiness that go with it, you must consciously choose to dwell on your strengths most of the time.

You Are a Bundle of Resources

One of the most obvious characteristics of leaders in public life is that they view themselves as bundles of resources that can be utilized in many different ways, like a tool can be used to achieve different results. Leaders are adamant about applying themselves only in those areas in which they can perform well and make a significant difference. They focus only on those areas in which they can succeed because of their special talents.

One of the best questions you can ask yourself, over and over, is "What can I, and only I, do that, if done well, will make an extraordinary difference in my situation?"

The law of concentration also says that all great success in life comes from single-minded, focused concentration on doing one thing or a few things extremely well. Success comes from staying at a particular task, the most valuable and important task you could be doing, until you succeed.

Every great human achievement is preceded by an extended period of dedicated, concentrated effort. However, there is little to be gained by digging determinedly, if you're digging in the wrong place. As Benjamin Tregoe, management consultant, said, "The very worst use of time is to do well what need not be done at all."

Assess Your Strengths and Weaknesses

This brings us to the importance of self-assessment with regard to your strengths. When we do strategic planning for corporations, we deal continually with what is called concentration of power. Where does and where can the company focus and concentrate its resources to achieve extraordinary results in a competitive market?

We start from the viewpoint that a company has a certain degree of flexibility in determining what it offers to justify its existence in the marketplace. We say that the purpose of a business is to create and keep a customer. The customer or the person that the company is organized to serve in some way is central to every calculation and every decision. We put the imaginary customer in the middle of the table and strategically plan with him or her in mind.

Increase Your Return on Energy

The critical issue in corporate strategic planning is to increase the *return on equity* invested in the corporation. It is to allocate and deploy assets in such a way that the rewards that the company earns are greater than they would be in the absence of the planning exercise. We start off with establishing clear values, a clear vision of what the company wants to become in the future, and a written mission statement that describes the strategic objective and positioning for the company.

Each person needs to do the same for him- or herself. The purpose of your *personal strategic planning* is to enable you to increase your return on energy. Because your time is your life, and your mental, emotional, and physical energies are your most valuable resources, your job is to organize your efforts in such a way as to give you maximum rewards and satisfaction for your energy invested.

Differentiate Yourself

Each company and each product or service either has or must develop a *unique selling proposition*. This is the key to differentiating the company and the company's products and services from the competition. Often, this is called a competitive advantage. Sometimes we call it an area of superiority.

In every case, it is essential to determine how, where, why, and in what degree a particular company or product differs from every other company that is competing with it for the right to create and keep customers in that market niche. What applies to competitive businesses applies to you, too.

You Are the President of You, Inc.

You are the president of your own life. You are the president of your own personal services corporation. You are in business for yourself. You are self-employed. No matter who signs your paycheck, you are working for yourself from the day you take your first job to the day you retire.

You may work at someone else's office or company, but you are always self-employed. The failure of many people to recognize this fact of self-employment and to behave as though this were true is a major reason for low self-confidence, underperformance, unhappiness, and failure in working life.

As the president of your own company, selling your services in the marketplace to the highest bidder, you are completely responsible for identifying your own unique selling proposition.

What is it that you do *better* than *anyone* else? Why are you *special* or different? What is your area of *competitive advantage?* If you had to write, in 25 words or less, exactly why someone should hire and promote and pay you to do a particular job, rather than hire, promote, and pay someone else, what would you point out as your *area of superiority?*

Join the Top 3 Percent

Many people have a tough time with this question. What matters at this point, though, is that you are asking the question at all. The very fact that you are thinking this way is moving you rapidly into the top 3 percent of working Americans. Only the top 3 percent see themselves as self-employed and self-responsible, and they are the most respected and important people in any organization.

Your first question is, What am I really good at today? What is my personal area of competitive advantage or superiority in my current job?

We are all responsible for asking and answering these questions for ourselves, today and throughout our careers. No one else can or will do it for us.

The amount of knowledge in every field is doubling every two to three years. Your skills are becoming obsolete at a more rapid rate than ever before, and new skills are essential for survival, not to mention success in highly competitive markets.

If your knowledge and skill isn't doubling every two to three years in your field, you will soon be out of your business, and some-one else will have your job. Whatever got you to where you are today is not enough to get you any further, as the title of Marshall Goldsmith's best-selling book, *What Got You Here Won't Get You There* (Writers of the Round Table Press, 2011), suggests. This is an inevitable and unavoidable fact of working life.

Designing Your Future

Your next question is, What *could* my area of competitive advantage be? Of all the areas in which I might be able to develop an area of superiority and become really good, taking my values and goals into consideration, what could it be?

The final question, perhaps the most important question on this subject, is the question, What should my area of competitive advantage be?

If you could be really excellent at any one skill sometime in the future, what one skill would help you the most to move to the top of your field? Imagine that you have no limitations on what you could learn and master. To accelerate your career, what *should* you really be good at some time in the future?

Find Out What You Are Meant to Do

A friend of mine built a company and sold it a couple of years ago. He had money in the bank and he decided to change careers. He had lots of time to think about it and to make the right choice. He went to an industrial psychologist and took an entire battery of tests; he underwent several interviews to find out what he was ideally suited to do in a new career.

At the end of this process, his friend, the industrial psychologist, sat him down and told him that his greatest strengths were consulting and presenting professional development seminars for managers and sales people.

My friend got a little bit angry. He said, "But you know that I'm afraid to speak on my feet in front of a group! You know that it makes me nervous and I become tense even thinking about it."

His friend said, "Yes, I know that's true. But you didn't ask me to tell you what would be convenient and easy for you to do. You asked me to tell you that would be the right thing for you to do. And the area where you have the greatest potential strength at this time is in consulting and training managers and sales people."

Be Prepared to Develop New Skills

My friend realized that what he was saying was true. He then went out and took courses in which he learned to overcome his fear of public speaking. He learned how to give presentations to a professional audience. It didn't take long, and six months later he began his own consulting and training business. He is now doing extremely well and he's never been happier in his life.

It often happens that your strengths are like muscles, undeveloped and requiring a long period of exercise to build up to the point where you can begin to win competitions. Michael Jordan said: "Everybody has talent, but to translate it into ability takes hard work."

A journey of a thousand leagues begins with a single step. You start by sitting down and setting goals for yourself. You decide where you are now and where you want to be at a specific time in the future. What additional knowledge and skills will do the most to help you to increase your return on energy invested? In what areas will a particular skill be useful and valuable to you and enable you to stand out from others?

Be Aware of Yourself

The key to becoming a fully functioning, fully integrated personality, the basic factors underlying self-confidence, is for you to become more aware of who you really are, and what you really want in life.

Sometimes, as a result of looking inward, you will discover opportunities for great breakthroughs in your life that you may never have seen before. You begin with the process of self-disclosure. In determining your strengths for the future, you begin to engage in a search process to explore all the different areas in which you may have hidden talents. One form of self-disclosure is to fill out a series of questionnaires and tests that examine parts of your personality and skills of which you might be unaware.

Invest in Yourself

Some years ago, I personally went to an industrial psychologist and took a battery of tests to find out my strengths and weaknesses. Much of my adult life has been affected by what came out of those tests. The tests pointed to areas in which I had natural talents and abilities. They also revealed my personality weaknesses and areas in which I had little interest or ability.

These tests, such as the DISC/Values Assessment, can do the same for you. They reveal a lot about you. They tell you what you like and enjoy, and what sort of work you will find most fulfilling. They tell you your true values and major motivators, and what areas of activity will make you the happiest. Their results can save you years of hard work in the wrong job.

If you have the time and the money, a detailed process of personality and career counseling is a very valuable exercise that can have a major influence on the rest of your career. If you lack either the time or the money, there are many books full of self-grading tests available in the bookstores. You can take these tests yourself, and they will give you very accurate feedback. There are several companies that have developed entire batteries of self-grading assessment instruments, each of which can give you insights into your strengths and weaknesses in particular areas.

Self-Analysis and Self-Disclosure

There are also a series of exercises in self-analysis and self-disclosure that you can complete yourself with just a pen and paper. These exercises can often open your eyes and help you to see possibilities that may surprise you.

The first exercise is for you to realize that you have already done many things and played many roles in life. Starting in childhood, you have learned how to do and perform a remarkable variety of tasks. You have a tremendous number of skills and talents that you have developed over time, many of which you simply take for granted.

Once, some years ago, I applied for a job as an extra in a movie. On the application form, one of the questions asked was, "What skills do you have that might make you more valuable as an extra in different scenes in the movie?"

They gave me a checklist of about 200 different things that a person might be called on to do in a movie. My job was to tick off all the activities with which I had had previous experience. As I went down the list, I still remember being astonished at the incredible number of things that I had learned to do, without even thinking about it.

They ranged from a variety of sports, to driving a variety of vehicles, to riding horses, to holding babies, to washing dishes, climbing ladders, swinging on ropes, swimming, diving, jumping, tumbling on the ground, and on and on. Perhaps one of the reasons that so many people have such low self-confidence is because they have never sat down to make up a list of how talented and capable they really are.

List All Your Current Skills and Capabilities

The first exercise for you is to write down a list of everything that you do on a regular basis. Write out all your roles and the parts you play, from the time you get up in the morning, until the time you go to bed at night. If you play sports or exercise with various equipment, write them out. If you are a parent, cook, a dishwasher, a driver, a shopper, a reader, a writer, a worker performing various jobs, a buyer, a seller, a negotiator, a teacher, a manager, a salesperson, a typist, a telephone-answering person, and whatever else you can think of, write it down. Be as detailed as possible.

Walk through your day, minute by minute and hour by hour, and write out everything that you do over the course of a day, a month, and a year. When you've completed this list, you will be astonished at how many skills you have developed and which you use on a regular basis.

Cluster Your Roles and Activities

The second part of this self-disclosure and self-analysis exercise is for you to make a new list on which you begin to *cluster* the various things you do into categories. One of your categories may be parenting. Under the parenting heading, write down all the things you do as a parent that are part of parenting. As a wife or husband, write down everything you do as a wife or husband, which you perhaps would not do if you were not married.

If you are a manager or a sales person, or if you hold any other position, write down everything that you do in your job, day in and day out. You might use a heading entitled friend, and under this heading you would write all the things that you do as a friend. Phone people, visit, write letters, socialize, go out for dinner, meet after work, and so on. If you play sports, put sports as a heading and write down all the physical activities that you engage in. If you are interested in reading, write down all the subjects that you read about on a regular basis.

Set Priorities on Your Roles

When you have completed clustering all your roles and activities into groups, the final step in this exercise is to set *priorities* on each group. Which group of activities is most important to you? Which group of activities is second most important to you? If you were going to be sent to a desert island for an indefinite term, and you could only take two or three of these activities with you, which ones would they be?

When you have numbered your clusters, or groups, by priority, you will have created a very clear picture of who you are and what is valuable to you in life.

Your next questions might be:

1. What do I need to do in each of these areas in order to get the very most satisfaction and enjoyment from this area?
2. What do I need to do more of or less of?
3. What do I need to get into or get out of?
4. What is more important within each cluster and what is less important?
5. If I had to choose, how would I choose and select among the various things I do?

You will be amazed at the kind of answers you start to come up with. In my experience, you will first be surprised at the clusters that appear at the top of your list, and then by the clusters, some of which take up an enormous amount of your time, that are not really very important to you at all. For you to really know yourself, you have to take the time to analyze yourself like this on paper.

Ask for Input from Others

A second exercise that is very helpful in learning more about yourself, and one that has been a turning point in the lives of many people, is to turn to someone close to you and ask him or her what they think you should do with your life.

Ask a person you trust what he or she thinks are your strong points and your weak points, your strengths and vulnerabilities? What advice would someone who cares about you give to you about the kind of work you should be doing and the kind of talents you should be developing?

Even people who don't know you very well will often be able to give you insights about yourself and your possibilities that will be extremely accurate and might even be in areas you haven't even thought about.

Once, I was driving with a business associate to an appointment that was some way out of town. We had a chance to talk as we were driving along, and I was wrestling with what I should do at the next stage of my career. I was seriously considering getting into the business of professional speaking and giving seminars and eventually producing audio programs. On a lark, I turned to him and asked him, in all honesty, "If I were going to change careers, what do you think I would be good at?"

An Important Insight

My associate sat and thought for a while and then he turned to me and said, "Brian, I think you would be very good at speaking and training and giving seminars. You do a lot of reading and research, and you seem to enjoy sharing your ideas with other people. The best use of your time would be to share your ideas with audiences."

Until then, I had seldom spoken publicly, and I had never given a seminar before. I won't say that that incident was the turning point for me, but it was the final assurance that I needed to make the decision to become a professional speaker and trainer. This business associate, a casual acquaintance, could see it clearly.

Today, I address more than 250,000 people each year all over the United States, Canada, Europe, Asia, Australia, and New Zealand. I've spoken on every island in the Caribbean and in Mexico. It must have been the right decision.

Determine What Motivates You

A third method of self-analysis is to apply the work of Dr. David McClelland of Harvard to assessing your own areas of greatest potential.

McClelland developed a method of interviewing people to find out what sort of jobs they would be best at. His conclusion is that people fall into *three* basic categories. You can usually tell whether a person will be suited to a particular job by finding out whether they fall into one of these three areas.

The method of interviewing, which you can do on *yourself*, consists of asking the job candidate detailed questions about previous peak experiences or moments of personal pride in his or her past.

The categories were determined by analyzing what most motivates a person. What are the sorts of activities that a person most enjoys and has been most successful at in their previous life and work? There are basically three motivational profiles, and each person falls into one of them, as do you.

The Achiever Profile

The first is what is called the achiever profile. The achiever is a person whose greatest sense of accomplishment comes from achieving something that is almost exclusively an *individual* activity. A person who enjoys climbing a mountain, or completing a course of study, or running a race, or overcoming any obstacle to win through by him- or herself would be classified as an achiever.

There are specific strengths that achievers have and specific jobs that achievers would be best at. One of these would be in the field of *selling*. Because selling is an individual activity, the people who are the very best at selling are those who most enjoy individual activities and individual accomplishment.

The Leader Profile

The second type of motivation is that of power. A person with a strong power orientation is one who enjoys getting things done through others. Power in this context refers to being able to influence and coordinate the activities of others over a period of time to complete a complex task. A coach of a sports team or a manager at work who really enjoys what he or she is doing would be a person who is most motivated by this kind of power or influence.

The Affiliation Profile

The third kind of motivation is called affiliation. A person with an affiliation motivation is one who most enjoys working harmoniously with other people as part of a team. This person enjoys both supporting others and being supported by others. He or she enjoys cooperating with others toward a common goal and seeing the goal achieved successfully.

Questions to Ask

When you apply this test to yourself, you ask yourself:

1. What do I like to do more than anything else?
2. What have I done in the past that has given me my greatest feelings of self-esteem and personal pride?
3. What have been my personal peak experiences in life?

Whatever you seem to have enjoyed the most is a good indication of where your strengths lie. Your strengths may be completely hidden, but by asking yourself these questions and facing the answers unblinkingly, you will begin to uncover them. When you uncover a potential strength in yourself and begin to develop it so that you can use it in your life, you begin to feel really terrific about yourself.

Make a Real Difference

Your most important job is to apply yourself where you can make the greatest positive difference. This will be the area where you get your highest *return on energy*. When you are working and expanding your capabilities in an area of your greatest strengths, you feel terrific about yourself. You feel like a winner. You enjoy wonderful feelings of self-confidence and self-esteem.

Accept Your Weaknesses

In almost any area, it is also important for your happiness that you develop a proper perspective on the inevitable weaknesses that you may have. Here are some insights that may be helpful to you.

The first insight is that almost every weakness can be viewed as a strength inappropriately applied. If you use one of your strengths where it is neither required nor helpful, it actually can be a weakness if it interferes with your ability to get the result you desire.

Sales versus Management

I had a gentleman working for me at one time who was direct and extremely aggressive. He started in sales and was very successful, and then he was promoted into a management position. As a manager, his aggressiveness made him the kind of person that no one wanted to deal with.

What I had forgotten was that his major skills lay in selling, in an area of *individual* achievement. His aggressiveness was a strength in selling, but it was a weakness when he was put into a management position in which his strength could not be used properly.

Many of the so-called weaknesses that you might have are merely strengths being used in the wrong place and for the wrong purposes.

Situational Weaknesses

A weakness may simply be *situational*. There is an old saying, "When you go into the woods, you must expect the mosquitoes." Sometimes you will be criticized for the things you do, and you may conclude that you are weak in these areas. However, it may be that criticism just comes with the territory.

I speak on sales, management, and motivation to a great number of people. Occasionally, people come up to me or write and tell me that they didn't like my talk. Even though more than 99 percent of the e-mails and letters that I receive are highly favorable, there are inevitably people who, for some reason, are not happy. These are the inevitable mosquitoes that go along with my profession.

You will find that there are inevitable complaints and criticisms that go along with whatever you do. They may not be indicative of a weakness at all, but, rather, merely opinions or observations by another person.

You May Be Hypersensitive

You may have a personality weakness that has been caused by a previous experience. Someone may have taken advantage of you in the past, and you may be hypersensitive to being taken advantage of again in the future. You may have been raised with destructive criticism and have, therefore, developed a very thin skin as a result. The slightest suggestion that a person does not completely approve of your behavior might cause you to react negatively. This may be seen as a personality flaw or weakness, whereas, in reality it is merely a result of your previous reinforcement history. It may also be something that will be helpful for you to decide to get over.

Amenable to Education

Your weakness may be amenable to education. Often the only thing holding you back from extraordinary accomplishment is a little bit of learning. If you take the right courses, listen to the right audio programs, and read the right books, that may be all that you need to do to become exceptional in your field.

Your supposed weakness may be *irrelevant*. It may be that someone else expects you to have certain qualities and abilities that you simply don't have and that you are not interested in or capable of developing. Often the disappointment of others can cause you to feel that you are deficient in some way when, in reality, that particular skill or ability is not important to you anyway.

Weaknesses Are Good Indicators

Finally, what appears as a weakness can be a key indicator of the type of work or activity that you should *not* be engaging in. It may be that you don't enjoy that area of endeavor at all. If you try to do a job or task, and you consistently do it poorly, this may be a way of Nature telling you that this is the wrong field for you.

Strengths and Weaknesses

The most important point to remember with regard to your strengths and weaknesses is that everybody has both. There are areas in which you are strong, and there are areas in which you can become extraordinary in your performance. There are areas in which you are weak and you probably should not be spending any more time there than is necessary to assure yourself that you are good enough move ahead.

Take the time to analyze yourself carefully. By practicing self-disclosure, with yourself and others, both in written and spoken form, you will develop a higher level of self-awareness and self-honesty. As you become more knowledgeable about your strengths, you will become more self-accepting of whom you really are. As your level of self-acceptance increases and you begin to respect yourself for your unique talents and abilities, your level of self-esteem and self-confidence will go up as well.

When you minimize or downplay your weaknesses and simultaneously identify and maximize your strengths, you will become a peak performer in everything you decide to do.

Action Exercises

1. Decide today that you are going to become very good at what you do, that you are going to join the top 10 percent in your field.

2. Identify the most important skills you have, those skills that are most important to your doing an excellent job.

3. Determine your natural strengths and abilities, those jobs and tasks that you do well and most enjoy.

4. What is your competitive advantage? What is it that you do better than almost anyone else? What should it be? What could it be in the future?

5. What sort of work motivates you the most? What activities give you the greatest sense of personal satisfaction?

6. In what areas do you achieve your highest return on energy? What do you do that really makes a difference to yourself and your business?

7. Take some time with a pen and paper to complete one or more of the exercises explained in this chapter so you can be sure that you are doing exactly the right work for you.

CHAPTER
6

Triumphing over Adversity

The miracle. Or the power, that elevates the few to be found in their industry, application, and perseverance under the promptings of a brave, determined spirit.

—Mark Twain

True self-confidence comes from positive *knowing*, rather than positive thinking. Your goal should be to develop the kind of unshakable self-confidence that makes you an unstoppable force of nature. Your job is to take every step possible to make yourself so positive that you become irresistible and able to accomplish any goal that you set your mind to. One of the most important things you need is an absolute faith in your ability to overcome any adversity that the world can throw at you.

Persistence Is Essential

Napoleon Hill wrote that "Persistence is to the character of man, as carbon is to steel." He also said that "Before success comes in any man's life he is sure to meet with much temporary defeat and, perhaps, some failure. When defeat overtakes a man, the easiest and most logical thing to do is quit. That is exactly what the majority of men do."

In reality, your persistence is your measure of your belief in yourself and your ability to succeed. If you absolutely believe, without question, that if you persevere long enough and hard enough, you will ultimately win, then nothing will stop you. When you build within yourself this absolute assurance, then virtually anything becomes possible for you. Your self-confidence goes through the roof.

The Reality Habit

Robert Ringer, in his best-selling book, *Million Dollar Habits* (Fawcett, 1990), says that the most important of all the habits that lead to great achievement is what he calls the "reality habit." It explains the attitudes of men and women who have achieved greatness in almost every field.

Happy, successful people are intensely realistic. They do not allow themselves the luxury of self-delusion. They face the world as it is, rather than the way they wish it would be. They accept the unalterable facts of life as given, and they work and plan their activities around them.

In learning how to triumph over adversity, the application of the reality principle is to simply accept that "problems are inevitable." Problems, setbacks, and disappointments are an unavoidable reality of life. Your ability to deal with these difficulties has as much to do with your self-confidence as any other factor.

The Test of Character

It's easy to feel good about yourself and to have high levels of self-confidence when everything is going well, but the true test of a man or woman is when you can keep your head and continue to function when things seem to be falling down around you, and everyone else is discouraged and often blaming it on you. These are the times when you really show the kind of stuff you are made of.

The Stanford University Business School conducted extensive research into the qualities of a man or woman that mark him or her for advancement into the executive suite, and ultimately, to the position of president and chief executive officer. They used a variety of questionnaires, surveys, and tests, going back to when an individual first joined a large company, to find ways to predict which people would be most likely to rise to the top of a large organization.

After examining dozens of qualities, they were finally able to isolate two qualities that were most predictive of executive success, in terms of assuring that the organization under their control would continue to survive and thrive in a dynamic and competitive world.

Play Well on the Team

The first quality they identified was the ability to perform well as a member of a team, and the ability to put together teams to accomplish common objectives. All the business and the interpersonal skills that make a person valuable to an organization seem to be demonstrated in a team setting. This quality was relative easy to observe and measure over the course of a person's career.

Crisis Management

The second quality they identified was harder to measure, even though it was absolutely indispensable for long-term, high-level success. This quality was the ability to function well in a *crisis.*

Napoleon called this "four o'clock in the morning courage," the kind of courage that is instantly available to a person woken up at that time, who has no time to prepare mentally and emotionally for a crisis. He called this the rarest form of courage, and, in his conclusion, very few people had it.

In military terms, they call this being under fire. A question that all soldiers, sailors, and airmen wonder about is how they and others will perform under fire. They know that this is the ultimate test of the character and training of an individual.

Organizations know that, often, their very survival will depend on how well an individual deals with the inevitable, unexpected reversal of fortune. The Stanford study concluded that, although this quality was hard to measure because a real crisis could not be anticipated or created for test purposes, it was still critical in predicting success in the higher levels of the business.

Reversals of Fortune

This is also true for you. Your self-esteem and self-confidence is closely tied to your deep inner feeling about your ability to be effective when faced with problems and difficulties that hit you like a punch in the solar plexus. It is your ability to pick yourself up from the mat and keep on swinging that is the real measure of what you are made of.

One of my favorite poems is *The Quitter* by Robert W. Service. There is a verse in that poem that goes like this:

> You're sick of the game, well that's a shame,
> You're young and you're strong and you're bright:

You've had a raw deal! I know, but don't squeal,
Buck up, do your damnedest and fight.
It's the plugging away that will win you the day,
So don't be a piker, old pard;
Just draw on your grit, it's easy to quit,
It's the keeping your chin up that's hard.

The quality of your entire personality is affected by how you deal with adversity, how well you keep your chin up. Successful and self-confident people are not those who do not have problems, they are merely those who deal with their problems in a more effective way than the average person.

B.C. Forbes, the founder of *Forbes* magazine, wrote that "History has demonstrated that the most notable winners usually encounter heartbreaking obstacles before they triumphed. They won because they refused to become discouraged by their defeat." So can you.

The Challenge-Response Theory

In 1952, historian Arnold Toynbee was nominated for the Nobel Prize, largely as the result of his work in studying the life cycles of civilizations. He estimated that, in human history, there had been 21 great civilizations, 20 of which had broken down over time. He considered the American civilization to be the 21st.

His writings were meant to illuminate and give guidance to modern historians and politicians so that they could better assure the survival and success of their nations, and in the case of the United States, the perpetuation of the American Republic.

Toynbee postulated what he called the challenge-response theory of history. He said that every large civilization began as a small group of people that eventually found itself facing a challenge from the outside. In most cases, this challenge was composed of enemy forces bent on its destruction. However, in some cases, the challenges came from the weather or geography.

Deal with the Challenge Effectively

When faced with a challenge, if the small group of people responded in a positive and constructive way, they would overcome the challenge and, in so doing, they would grow. In growing, this group or tribe would trigger another, even larger challenge, usually aggression from other tribes.

Once again, the group would have to reorganize itself internally to face the even larger challenge. If it again responded in a positive and constructive way, and overcame the challenge, it would continue to grow. At each stage of growth, the size of the tribe, nation, or state would trigger ever greater challenges.

At each stage, as long as the civilization continued to respond effectively to the challenge, it continued to grow. The turning point came when the civilization no longer had the will or ability to rise to the challenge of the time, and as a result, it began to decline and was eventually swept away by the events of history.

All Civilizations Eventually Decline

Sometimes, as in the case of the Roman civilization, it took several hundred years before Rome faded as a major Mediterranean power. Once the Roman people became addicted to "bread and circuses" and various forms of government welfare and handouts, they lost their will to resist the external challenges represented by the barbarian tribes from the north.

Sometimes, the civilization fell rather quickly. In less than five years from his landing at Vera Cruz, Cortez was able to destroy the foundation of the Aztec civilization that had endured for hundreds of years. The centuries-old Austro-Hungarian Empire, weakened from within, fell apart in the four short years of World War I, and it never recovered.

However long the period of decline, the critical event was always the loss of will and the inability to rise to the external threat or difficulty. Toynbee concluded that with very few exceptions, civilizations decline from within before they are conquered from without.

The Story of Your Life

The reason that Toynbee's theory is so relevant to us is that it explains much of our lives. No matter how well our parents protect us while we are growing up, sooner or later we face challenges and difficulties in our relationships, our work, and in our other activities. Each time we face one of these external challenges, we have the choice of either responding positively and constructively, or of letting it overwhelm us.

If we choose deliberately to respond in a positive and constructive way, to keep our minds calm and cool, and deal effectively with the inevitable problem, we learn and grow and become stronger. Our self-confidence goes up. Our belief in our ability to achieve our goals increases. Our self-esteem rises. We develop a better self-image and we become more self-assured, confident, and optimistic.

The Rise and Fall of a Business

Every small and large company goes through the same cycle of challenge and response. If a small company is capable of rising to the inevitable setbacks and reversals it experiences, it continues to grow, and in so doing, it triggers even greater challenges, reversals, and setbacks. Peter Drucker said, "A company stays in business as long as it continues to make enough money to pay for its mistakes."

One business consultant estimated that, every three months, a small business has a crisis that, if not responded to properly, will lead to the collapse of the enterprise.

You and I are similar to small businesses in many respects. Fortunately, an inability to respond will not lead to something as final as a business collapse. However, if for any reason, we don't get on top of the challenges but instead let them get on top of us, our self-esteem and self-confidence will decrease and our ability to deal with subsequent difficulties will diminish dramatically.

Your Responses Determine Your Future

Almost everything that happens to you is determined by your responses to the ups and downs of daily life. Your responses are the result of everything you have learned and experienced over time. Thomas Huxley said, "Experience is not what happens to a man; it is what a man does with what happens to him."

Your life, and everything about you, is demonstrated in the way you react. It's not in what happens to you; it is how you respond to it. This is why the Stanford study was quite clear about this quality when it stated that "The proven ability to function in a crisis is the absolute prerequisite for promotion to a senior position."

In a way, what we are really talking about here is *character*. One of your aims in life should be to develop your character, to become a better, finer, and stronger human being. The development of character, essential to your long-term happiness and well-being, requires that you go through the crucible of setback and temporary defeat and emerge victorious.

Problems and Difficulties Come Unbidden

You probably make every effort to organize your life in such a way that you minimize the unexpected and usually unpleasant surprises that may occur. You use your intelligence, education, and experience to arrange your life and affairs so that you avoid adversity wherever and whenever possible.

You probably plan and prepare carefully in advance to assure that things go smoothly, at home and at work. You are especially careful with your health, and with the well-being of members of your family. You are thoughtful about the things that you can do to assure a greater likelihood of success in your business or career. You lock doors, insure properly, drive carefully, and otherwise reduce your potential exposure to unhappy events.

Almost everyone does this, except for those who are thoughtless and irresponsible. Yet, in spite of making every effort to avoid adversity, you experience adversity nonetheless. Adversity comes to you "unbidden." You tend to be "blindsided" by adversity. It befalls you in spite of your very best efforts to the contrary.

Adversity and Character Development

In the absence of adversity, however, you cannot develop a stronger character. You cannot become a better person. You cannot develop resilience, perseverance, and resoluteness of personality. You cannot develop into the kind of person who enjoys high levels of self-confidence, and a feeling that you can meet and master whatever you are faced with. You cannot grow stronger without the adversity that you so conscientiously avoid.

Caught in this conundrum, you have only one choice. You can choose, in advance, to be equal to the occasion. Ann Landers summed it up beautifully in these words, "If I were asked to give what I consider the single most useful bit of advice for all humanity, it would be this: expect trouble as an inevitable part of life, and when it comes, hold your head high, look it squarely in the eye and say, 'I will be bigger than you, you cannot defeat me.'"

Your Response-Ability Is the Key

Frederick Robertson said, "It is not the situation that makes the man, but the man who makes the situation." It is not what happens to you, but how you respond to what happens to you, that determines your whole life. In the responses chosen are contained the determining factors of human greatness or depravity. Great men and women are simply those who have responded well when the chips were down, and the rest is history.

Dr. Abraham Zaleznik of Harvard is one of the few people who has ever done extensive research into the subject of *disappointment*. What he found, in studying the way that different people respond to disappointment, was that you could largely tell how high and how far a person was going to go in life by simply observing how they reacted when they faced frustration and setbacks in reaching their goals.

Dr. Zaleznik found that the great majority of people do not prepare mentally for the inevitable disappointments that come in life, and when they arrive, they tend to be taken off guard and emotionally overwhelmed. They then generalize these disappointments and allow themselves to feel that, because they have not succeeded, they are not really very good at what they do.

They tend to interpret these disappointments as being indicative of their lack of ability and competence. As a result, they become easily disappointed in themselves, and they lose the courage and confidence that they need to press forward. Often they become depressed, and in the majority of cases, they gradually give up. They stop setting goals and working on themselves and become more concerned about security and potential loss than about taking chances and potential gain.

Responding Well to Disappointment

The high achievers in his study responded to disappointment very differently from the low achievers. First, they mentally prepared for a disappointment, in advance, so that when it arrived, they had already given some thought to how they would react and to the possible courses of action open to them.

They regard a particular setback as being specific to a particular situation and not being indicative of a general lack of ability or of a character flaw. More than anything else, top men and women had developed a series of mental tools that they used almost automatically whenever things went wrong for them.

Crisis Anticipation

Napoleon Bonaparte is considered by historians to have been perhaps the most brilliant battlefield general in human history. In a military career spanning 25 years and involving hundreds of battles, large and small, he lost only *three* battles. It was said that his very presence on the battlefield was worth an additional 40,000 soldiers to the French army because of the boost in morale that it gave them.

Napoleon was famous for taking the time to study the battle-field and to think through every possible eventuality of the pending battle. He prepared with no illusions and with an attitude that dealt with the worst possibilities and reverses that could occur.

When the battle was underway, and confusion reigned everywhere, a steady stream of messengers and officers would come to him with news and messages, requesting instructions on what to do next. His responses were always clear, concise, and immediate. No matter what happened, he had an order and an answer at the tip of his tongue. The reason for this, and what helped to make him the master of all of Europe, was because he had thought everything through in advance.

Advance Thinking and Planning

This book, *The Power of Self-Confidence*, is meant to be practical and helpful to you. In the coming pages, I will share with you some of the best mental tools used by the most effective men and women in our society to cope with adversity.

What I suggest is that you study them, turn them over in your mind, and review them regularly until they become an automatic part of your thought processes. When they do, I promise that you will take a giant step toward becoming unstoppable and toward enjoying the high levels of self-confidence that are possible for you.

The Concept of Failure

The first mental technique is for you to reassess your entire attitude toward the concept of failure. You know that the "fear of failure" is the greatest single obstacle to success and happiness in adult life. You also know that this is a conditioned response that originated in early childhood as the result of destructive criticism and other mistakes that your parents made in bringing you up. Fortunately, it is a learned fear, and because of this, it can be unlearned, thereby freeing you from the fears that hold you back and giving you the self-confidence that propels you forward.

The starting point of eliminating this fear is for you to accept and realize that no success is possible without failure. All success is preceded by failure, usually great failure, repeated over a long period of time.

Abraham Lincoln was considered one of the great failures of American politics, a man who lost his business, lost his sweetheart, and was defeated for election over and over again. However, by learning from every defeat, he won the final election and became one of the most important and respected presidents we have ever had.

As Stanley Judd wrote, "Don't be afraid to fail. Don't waste energy trying to cover up failure. Learn from your failures and go on to the next challenge. It's ok to fail. If you're not failing, you're not growing."

Double Your Rate of Failure

You only learn how to succeed by failing, and no success is possible without it. A young journalist who asked him how he could be more successful faster once visited Thomas J. Watson. Watson, the founder of IBM, replied with these wonderful words, "Do you want to be successful? Then, double your rate of failure. Success lies on the far side of failure."

Every man or woman of great achievement has been, at one time, a magnificent failure. The greatest successes of our generation and of our history books are the stories of men and women who failed so many times that they finally learned how to succeed.

On the *David Susskind Show* some years ago, they had four men who had all become entrepreneurial millionaires before the age of 35. They were asked, during a break, to add up and calculate the total number of different businesses that they had started or tried before they found the business in which they made their fortunes. It turned out that the four men had started an average of 17 businesses each, an average of 16 of which had been unsuccessful, but it was the 17th business that had made them rich.

Now the obvious question is this: Did those young men fail in each of their previous business enterprises? The answer is clear. They did not fail. They were learning how to succeed. Their previous business enterprises were the testing grounds at which they learned the lessons necessary to achieve financial independence later.

Our Greatest Inventor

Thomas Edison was the most successful inventor of the 20th century, or of any century. He developed not only the electric light bulb, but the electric power company that made it possible to sell and deliver electric current and sell electric light bulbs to every city, town, and village in America. He patented more than one thousand devices at the U.S. Patent Office, almost all of which were brought into commercial production within his lifetime. Our way of life, and the way of life of almost everyone in the world, has been profoundly affected by his successes in the area of invention.

However, Thomas Edison was also an extraordinary failure as an inventor. He failed more times than any other inventor of his age. He failed thousands and thousands of times in attempting to find the proper filament for the first electric light bulb. He failed thousands of times more in attempting to find the proper plant from which to draw natural rubber. In his laboratories at what is now known as General Electric, he brought together some of the finest scientific minds of the age so that they could dramatically increase the number and speed of their failures.

Success Is a Numbers Game

Edison knew that success is a numbers game. It is based on intelligent effort and the law of probabilities. If you try enough different things in enough different ways, and you learn from each test or failure, then you must inevitably be successful. The fear of failure, on the other hand, causes people to try fewer and fewer things, thereby lowering the probability that they will ever achieve anything of consequence.

In the same year that Babe Ruth hit more home runs than any other batter in America, he also struck out more than any other batter. When the ball was thrown, he swung with every ounce of strength he had, often spinning around and falling down on the ground as a result of his efforts. However, he also set an American baseball record that was not broken for decades, and he became a legend we still talk about today.

Henry Ford, who was bankrupt at the age of 40 and who went on to become one of the world's richest men, wrote, "Failure is just another opportunity to more intelligently begin again." Dr. Joyce Brothers wrote that "The person interested in success has to learn to view failure as a healthy, inevitable part of the process of getting to the top."

Learn from Every Failure

Your job is not to fear failure or to avoid failure so much that you also avoid success. Your job instead is to move forward and take intelligent risks, thinking them through in advance and learning everything you can as you go along. Zig Ziglar said that you can tell how high a building is going to be by looking at how deep they dig the foundation. The height to which you rise in life will always be determined by the depth of your own personal foundation, which is almost always the quality and quantity of your failures, and what you have become as a result of them.

Napoleon Hill wrote, "When defeat comes, accept it as a signal that your plans are not sound: rebuild those plans and set sail once more toward your coveted goal."

Dale Carnegie wrote, "The successful man will profit from his mistakes and try again in a different way."

The starting point of triumphing over adversity is to overcome the fear of failure, to the point at which you are willing to proceed boldly in the direction of your dreams. Whatever your emotions, fear, or desire, they control your decisions and everything you do.

When you write down clear goals and make detailed plans for their accomplishment, and then think about your goals all the time, you build up within yourself the "white hot heat" of desire that can eventually become so powerful that it overcomes any fear of failure that might hold you back.

The more you think, talk, and write about your goals, the more determined you become to make them a reality, and the more likely it is that you will push yourself forward to overcome the fears that might hold you back.

Plan for the Future

The second mental technique you can use to deal with adversity is called crisis anticipation, and it refers to your ability to think. Your mind is the most powerful tool that you have with which to apprehend reality. Everything you feel and all your reactions are initially determined by how you think about any subject. If you change the quality of your thinking, you change the quality of your life. This begins by applying your ability to think to your existing situation.

Crisis anticipation is the exercise of looking down the road, 6–12 months, and making a list of everything that could go wrong in the areas that are important to you. It is similar to what Napoleon did in anticipation of an upcoming battle.

If you're in business, make a list of all the problems that might arise that could threaten the survival of your business. If you're in sales, make a list of all the things that could happen that could dramatically decrease your sales volume. With regard to your family, or even when considering a family vacation, make a list of all of the unexpected events that could occur that would derail your plans and goals.

Spread the Risk

In one business I worked with, the owner found that more than 60 percent of the sales were coming from 2 of the 11 sales people. If one of those people quit—or worse, went to work for a competitor— the company's sales volume would decline dramatically, and its ability to survive might actually be threatened.

Once the owner was clear about this, he immediately began an intensive sales training program for all his people. Simultaneously, he began recruiting and looking for better sales people while making arrangements to encourage his poor performers to go elsewhere. Within six months, no single sales person accounted for more than 15 percent of the business. And when it happened that one of his previous top sales people did decide to leave, the business was able to absorb the temporary drop in productivity and continue to grow.

What Could Go Wrong?

What are the likely crises that might occur in your life? What if interest rates doubled, or your business dropped by 50 percent? What if your best-selling products stopped selling or your best customers stopped buying? In what areas are you overly dependent on someone or something else for your continuing success? And what steps could you take, starting today, to guard against a crisis, should it occur? You will be amazed at how much more self-confidence you have when you have thought through the critical areas of your life and made plans in case something goes wrong.

Otto Von Bismarck, the "Iron Chancellor" of Germany, was considered to be one of the finest statesmen of the century. He was famous for always having what came to be called a Plan B for every situation. No matter what happened, and no matter how hard he had worked to bring about a particular result, if he was not successful, he could always reach into his drawer and pull out a fully developed backup plan ready to go. This habit of preparing for the unforeseen outcome led to him becoming one of the most powerful statesmen in Europe.

Become Intensely Solution Oriented

Think about the solution, about what can be done rather than what has happened and who is to blame. Don't waste a minute being upset or angry about something that has happened that cannot be changed.

Consciously choose the future over the past. Become intensely solution oriented rather than problem oriented. Think about what can be done immediately to resolve the difficulty. Look for the valuable lesson you can learn from this situation. Think how you can minimize the damages and maximize any opportunities that might arise out of this setback. As Friedrich Nietzsche, the philosopher, once said, "What doesn't kill me makes me stronger."

The only real antidote to worry and negativity is positive, purposeful, constructive action in the direction of your goals. As soon as you take action, your self-esteem and self-confidence start to increase again. You begin to feel more in control of your emotions and of your life. You stop making excuses and you start making progress. You start thinking about how you can turn this situation to your advantage.

Never Consider the Possibility of Failure

In the final analysis, you triumph over adversity by having clear values, clear goals and plans, and complete control over your mind and your thinking. You win by thinking about winning all the time and refusing to consider the possibility of losing. You win by resolving to persist, no matter what the odds, no matter what happens, until you succeed. You recognize that persistence is a form of courage. It is the courage to endure in the face of adversity and disappointment, and it is the one quality that guarantees that ultimately you will be successful.

Calvin Coolidge, President of the United States, summed this up when he wrote, "Nothing in the world can take the place of persistence. Talent will not; nothing is more common than unsuccessful men with talent. Genius will not; unrewarded genius is almost a proverb. Education will not; the world is full of educated derelicts. Persistence and determination alone are omnipotent."

Courage and Persistence

Persistence is self-discipline in action. Each time you exert the self-discipline to persist in the face of adversity and disappointment, your self-esteem goes up. When you practice persistence, you build up your resistance to taking the easy way out. You create the friction that comes from going against your natural tendencies. You generate the heat that crystallizes your character at a new higher level.

And with this higher level of persistence, self-discipline, and character, your self-esteem, self-respect, and personal pride increase.

Your belief in yourself serves as a deep foundation of confidence on which you build a great life. You become more positive, more optimistic, and more unstoppable in everything you do. You do this because, as Churchill said, you "Never give up; never, never give up."

Action Exercises:

1. Identify one major adversity that you dealt with and recovered from. What did you learn that has helped you to become a better person?

2. Determine the worst possible thing that could happen in your business or career. What could you do now to minimize the negative effects if it did occur?

3. What are the three worst things that could happen in your personal and family life, and what could you do to prepare against them?

4. What are the three biggest mistakes you have made, and what did you learn from each one?

5. What is the most effective way you could respond to your biggest problem today?

6. In what areas should you be prepared to take action and move forward rather than playing it safe?

7. What one action will you take immediately to face your fears and move forward to the achievement of one of your most important goals?

CHAPTER 7

Self-Confidence In Action

Above all, be of a single aim; have a legitimate and useful purpose, and devote yourself unreservedly to it.

—James Allen

One of the most valuable exercises you can engage in, to accomplish any goal you can set for yourself, is to ask yourself, "What is my limiting step?" What is the one factor that determines the speed at which I achieve my goal, or whether I achieve it at all?

Your ability to identify your limiting step is one of the best demonstrations of your intelligence. Your capacity to eliminate this limiting step is one of the best demonstrations of your overall competence in achieving anything you want.

Self-Confidence Is Critical

In studying everything that has been written or said about personal success, the conclusion I came to was that your level of self-confidence is probably the critical factor in everything you accomplish. When you have enough self-confidence, you will try almost anything. Because success is largely a matter of averages, or probabilities, the more things you try, the more likely it is that you will achieve greatly.

For many years, Amoco Petroleum was famous among oil companies for having consistently developed and maintained higher levels of oil and gas reserves than any other major oil company. The president of Amoco was asked why his company was so successful in this area. He replied simply that, "We drill more holes."

They didn't purport to be better or smarter than their competitors. They just focused on drilling more wells, and by the law of averages, they ended up drilling more successful wells and becoming one of the most profitable oil companies in the world.

Try More Things

The same is true for you. When you set more goals, try more things, engage in more activities, and explore more opportunities, your probabilities of success increase dramatically. The only real limiting step that you might have is your level of self-confidence. When you reach the point at which you believe in yourself absolutely, the barriers that exist in your external world will not stop you.

The major obstacles to success always lie *within* the mind of the individual. They are not contained in external circumstances, situations or people. As soon as you win the inner battle, the outer battle seems to take care of itself.

The development of self-confidence has been the turning point in my own life. The reason I feel so strongly about the subject is because of what it has meant to me. The development of greater self-confidence has enabled me to go from rags to riches, from limited means and worries about money to national and international renown. I have been able to go from living in a small, rented, one-bedroom apartment and being deeply in debt, to living in a beautiful home on a golf course and driving a new Mercedes.

An Inauspicious Beginning

Talent and ambition have been very helpful, but without the development of self-confidence, my inborn abilities would have lain dormant and unused, as they did for many years.

Before I gained enough self-confidence to commit completely to my goals, I was going nowhere with my life. I started with few advantages. I came from a home with three younger brothers, and while I was growing up, we never seemed to have any money. My father was a good man, but he was not always employed. I remember from my earliest days that we could never afford anything.

My mother used to dress us by buying used clothes from the Goodwill and the St. Vincent De Paul Rescue Missions. We would wear pants and shirts that had been given away by other families. Sometimes the kids at school recognized that the clothes I was wearing were their old clothes that their parents had given away.

Christmas and birthdays were not occasions of great celebration. We had little to give and little to share.

Early Behavior Problems

I became a behavior problem at an early age. I see now that I was just rebelling against my upbringing, but at the time, I was a real problem for everyone around me. I was constantly being kicked out of classes for misbehavior. I was suspended or expelled from four schools during my junior high and high school years. I had the sorry distinction of being the worst behaved kid in school, with more detentions, demerits, and failed classes than any other kid in the 9th, 10th, 11th, and 12th grades. I learned later that my teachers had voted me "the most likely to end up in prison."

I began working at a young age. I worked at a part time job, and then full time jobs to earn my own money, buy my own clothes, and eventually get my own car. I worked as a dishwasher in a small hotel for eight hours a day during my 12th-grade year, and, although I didn't drop out of high school, I failed out.

Failure from the Beginning

I continued going to school until the year was over, but I failed six out of my last seven courses. During the graduation ceremonies, they allowed me to go up on the stage in a gown, in front of the audience, and receive a certificate from the principal. The person in front of me received a diploma. The person in back of me also received a diploma. What I got was a "leaving certificate." A leaving certificate is just a polite way for the school to say, "Goodbye, please don't ever come back."

Laboring Jobs

While many of my friends who had graduated from high school went on to university to complete their educations, I began working at laboring jobs. Over the next few years, I worked as a dishwasher and a kitchen helper. I worked in sawmills and factories. I worked on construction crews and as a laborer. In one job, I dug wells. That's when you start from the ground level and work down, rather than up.

I worked at washing cars and as a galley boy on a ship. I worked in gas stations and as a mechanic's helper. When I answered employment ads in the paper, I never even got a reply from anyone. My job applications were just thrown in the wastebasket. When I was 23 years old, I was an itinerant farm worker, sleeping on the hay in the farmer's barn, and getting up when it was pitch black to eat with the farmer's family before the workday started.

Selling from Door to Door

In my mid-20s, I was still drifting, and in order to eat, I began selling office supplies from door to door. I did poorly. From there, I went to selling other things. I remember making calls for an entire month without making a single sale. I lived on loans and charity from family and friends. I had virtually no possessions, very few clothes even, no money, no high-school diploma, no marketable skills, and no experience of any real value to anyone. I was going nowhere fast.

Meanwhile, all around me, I saw people my own age, and younger, who were doing well. They were wearing nice clothes, driving nice cars, and working at well-paying jobs. They were moving onward and upward in their careers. They had offices and some of them had staffs. Several of them had gotten married and had homes and families and cars and furniture and what appeared to be pretty good lives.

The Big Question

From the age of 15, I had been wondering why it was that some people were more successful than others? Although I wasn't making much progress on the outside, I continued to read and search for the answers to this question, and I began to experiment with some of the ideas I discovered.

My first turning point came when I realized that my problems at school and in getting along with other people were as a direct result of my own personality. I realized that, if I wanted things to change,

I would have to change. I began to understand that my unhappiness and anger and frustration at my childhood experiences had caused me to develop a negative personality that turned many people off.

I accepted that any change that was going to take place had to begin with me, and it was up to me alone. No one was going to do it for me. No one would help me. No one else really cared. If I wanted to be successful and popular with others, I would have to go to work on myself and become a different person.

The Big Turning Point

The second turning point came for me when I was poor and 20 years old, living in a one-bedroom apartment and working at a laboring job during the day. I realized that I was completely responsible for my life and everything that happened to me from then on. If I wasn't happy with my income, my work, my education, or my future prospects, it was up to me to go to work on myself and make the necessary changes. They wouldn't happen by themselves.

The Importance of Goals

The third turning point came for me when I discovered the importance of setting goals and of making clear decisions about what I really wanted in each area of my life. When I first stumbled across the subject of goals, I thought they were something that they had in sports. The idea of setting them for myself wasn't quite believable. I had so many problems and excuses that I felt that goal setting was really just an exercise in futility. It might be a pleasant entertainment, but nothing would come of it, considering my situation.

Because I had low self-esteem and limited self-confidence, the first goals I set were not very high. They were consistent with what we talked about in Chapter 2 of this book, but I looked on the exercise as more of an entertainment than as an important steppingstone to success.

I remember sitting in someone else's cheap hotel room many years ago. I took out a piece of hotel stationery, wrote out a series of goals, put deadlines on them, and then made a simple plan for accomplishing them. I promptly lost the sheet of paper, but exactly 31 days later, just as I had written, and as the result of a remarkable series of coincidences, my goals were all achieved. I was in my 20s at the time, and I still remember the feeling of astonishment I had at that time. I felt that I had learned about a secret power that I could use to accomplish almost anything.

Three Great Ideas

I had learned three important ideas. First, accept complete responsibility for yourself and for everything that you are and ever will be. Second, accept that you can change your situation only by going to work on yourself and learning the things you need to know to be better. Third, set clear goals with time lines for the things you want and then work every day to bring those goals into reality.

For the next few years, I used these ideas sporadically. Each time I did, I would experience a burst of success and progress. As soon as I achieved a modicum of success, I would abandon these ideas and go back to simply reacting and responding to whatever happened on a daily basis.

It took me several years before I finally began practicing these ideas consistently, along with many others that I've mentioned in this program. I then began to get results in a systematic and consistent way.

We Sabotage Ourselves

I learned later that our natural tendency is to work hard until we find a method or technique that works for us, whether in life, work, or relationships, and then, for some perverse reason, we promptly abandon the technique and go back to behaving in our old way, in a random and haphazard manner.

A mental exercise program, like goal setting and positive thinking, is very much like a physical exercise program. If you expect it to really work for you, you have to practice it persistently, every day, and keep at it indefinitely. When I began to apply these proven success principles to my life, and worked on them every day, I was able to bring about almost miraculous changes in every area of my life.

Here's the point. I learned, in retrospect, that the reason that I suffered so many frustrations and drifted away from using these principles so often was because I lacked self-confidence. My conscious mind told me that these principles made sense. However, my subconscious mind, my storehouse of memories and emotions and previous experiences, was telling me that I wasn't good enough and that success was not really for me. As my friend Zig Ziglar says, "I was engineered for success but programmed for failure." I wanted success on the outside, but I didn't believe I was capable of it on the inside.

You Can Develop Any Quality

The fourth turning point for me, and the reason that I have written this book for you, was my discovery that I could develop any quality that I thought was necessary for my success and happiness. I learned that, by hard work and repetition, I could overcome and override my feelings of inferiority and undeservedness and build up my feelings of self-esteem and self-confidence.

I could identify and then alleviate my own bottlenecks or limiting steps. By working on myself every day, I could build myself up into the high-achieving, happy person that I really wanted to be. By taking my foot off my own subconscious brakes and putting them onto my conscious accelerator, I could begin to move ahead rapidly in life. The key, the spark plug, was the conscious and purposeful development and maintenance of high levels of self-confidence, and the self-esteem that goes with it.

The Secret of Success

Every successful man or woman that I have ever talked to or read about has come to pretty much the same conclusion. By every measure, you have more talent and ability than you could use in 100 lifetimes. You, too, can step on the accelerator of your own potential and begin moving forward at a speed that will amaze you. Many people who have listened to my programs or gone through my seminars have come back to me and told me that they cannot believe how fast their lives began to improve when they began to apply these principles on a daily basis.

The Four Ds of Success and Self-Confidence

How do you infuse your whole life with the kind of self-confidence that makes everything possible for you? The answer is contained in what I call the four Ds, which determine success in anything you really want to accomplish.

The first D is desire. You must really want to become a totally self-confident human being. You must build up your desire by thinking about it and talking about it, and working on it all the time. Your desire must become so intense that it overrides your fears of failure, rejection, and inferiority, and it becomes the dominant emotion governing your behaviors. Intense desire is the starting point of all personality modification and goal attainment.

The second D is decision. You must make a do-or-die decision that you will go to work on yourself and keep at it until you achieve the kind of self-confidence that enables you to do, be, and say whatever you want. You must burn your mental bridges. Many people want things but they never make the clear, unequivocal decision that they are going to do what it takes to get them.

The third D is determination. Once you have started to make significant changes in the way you act, your internal gyroscope will try to take over and bring you back into your comfort zone, into your old ways of acting.

Sometimes, progress will be slow, and, often, you will see no progress at all. Nonetheless, you must persist in the positive and constructive behaviors that you know will lead to making you into the kind of person you wish to become. Your determination must be as unshakable as the self-confidence you desire.

The fourth D is discipline. Underlying and surrounding all great achievement in life is the quality of self-discipline. This is *the ability to make yourself do what you should do, when you should do it, whether you feel like it or not.* Every practice of self-discipline strengthens your discipline in every other area of your life.

As Napoleon Hill said, after more than 20 years of research into the lives of successful men and women, "Self-discipline is the master key to riches." It is self-discipline that makes everything else possible.

If you have the desire to change, the decisiveness to take action, the determination to persist on your forward track, and the discipline to make yourself do whatever you need to do, your self-confidence and your success are inevitable.

Positive Knowing versus Positive Thinking

We said earlier that self-confidence comes from positive *knowing* rather than from just positive thinking or hoping. It is only when you have a firm conviction or belief in your abilities, based on experience, that you really know that your self-confidence is not an act.

This is why every act of self-confidence builds your self-confidence. Every success you experience builds your self-confidence and your ability to achieve further successes. Every mental exercise that you engage in to improve and strengthen your personality, builds your self-confidence. Everything that you learn and practice from the lives of other self-confident people improves you own self-image, increases your self-esteem, and raises your self-confidence.

The Gallup Success Survey

Some years ago, in the mid-1980s, the Gallup organization conducted one of the most extensive surveys into the reasons for success ever conducted in America. They selected 1,500 men and women whose names and biographies had appeared in Marquis's *Who's Who in America*, the most prestigious register of noteworthy individuals in the country.

They asked them, at great length, what they felt were the reasons why they had become so well known and respected in their lifetimes. This group included Nobel Prize winners, university presidents, heads of Fortune 500 corporations, leading academics, writers, inventors, entrepreneurs, and even a high-school football coach, a man who continued to have a significant impact on the lives and personalities of the young people he trained.

Five Essential Success Qualities

After many months of research and interviews, they were able to isolate the five most important qualities for success and self-confidence in America. Their findings turned out to be consistent with virtually all the other research that's been done in this area.

Common Sense

The first and most important success quality was defined as, common sense. It is said that the average person has an enormous amount of common sense because he or she hasn't used any of it yet. Common sense seems to be something that a person accumulates as the result of experience over a long period of time.

Common sense was defined by the participants in this survey as the "ability to cut to the core of a matter, to recognize and deal with the essential elements of a problem or a situation, rather than getting sidetracked by smaller issues or symptoms."

Another definition of common sense was "The ability to learn from experience and then to apply those lessons to subsequent experiences." Common sense was seen as a core quality that enabled a person to become increasingly more effective over time.

Wisdom Is Essential

Perhaps another word for common sense is *wisdom*. Aristotle once defined wisdom as an equal combination of *experience plus reflection*. He suggested that you need to, first, have the experience and, second, take an equal amount of time to think about what happened to you and what you could learn from it.

You are far, far wiser than you know. In fact, based on your experience, you probably have the ability to be far more effective than you are just by applying what you have already learned. The problem for most people is that they simply do not take enough time for *reflection*. They do not take the time to sit, write, think, and dialogue with others about their experiences.

Socrates once said that "We only learn something by dialoguing about it." You only really understand something to the degree to which you can discuss it with others or explain it to a third party. Your ability to translate your experience into words, which only comes through thinking and reflection, is essential for your growth and wisdom and common sense.

Gain Additional Knowledge

I would add one more ingredient to Aristotle's definition of wisdom, and that would be knowledge. Wisdom comes from equal parts knowledge, experience, and reflection. First you learn, then you practice what you learn, then you take time to think about what happened. When you turn off the television or radio, or put down the newspaper, and begin spending more time talking and thinking about what has happened to you, you begin to grow at an exponential rate.

Two Magic Questions

Perhaps the two best questions I have learned for personal growth are these: After every experience, successful or unsuccessful, stop and do an instant replay of the experience, preferably on paper, and ask yourself first, What did I do right? and second, What would I do differently?

If you take a piece of paper and write at the top of the page, What did I do right? and then write down every single part of the experience that you did correctly, you will be accelerating your development of common sense. By analyzing your immediate past performance, like football players do on video, you will find yourself improving at a rapid rate. The very fact that you take time to reflect will cause you to improve in the areas you pay attention to.

When you ask, What would I do differently? you begin to see all kinds of possibilities for improvement. The wonderful thing about these two questions is that the answers to both are positive and constructive. And when you dwell on the positive, constructive parts of your performance, present and future, these ideas sink deeper into your subconscious mind and program you to act in a manner consistent with that information the next time out.

Review Your Performance

One famous football coach would sit down with his better players and replay videos of their last games. He showed them running or passing or catching on the video, but without comment. The players, whose egos were very sensitive, were quite aware of their mistakes and weaknesses. Nothing needed to be said. As a result of reviewing the videos together, the players became better and better, and the coach was seen to be a great builder of men.

After every sales call or interview, do an instant replay, alone or with someone else, and ask yourself quickly, What did I do right? and What would I do differently? You will be amazed at what you see and how fast you begin to improve. This simple method will probably assure that you make more progress in one month than the average person makes in a year, or even two years. Just try it for one day and prove it to yourself.

Be Good at What You Do

The second quality for success and self-confidence that came out of the study was that of expertise. I talked about this at great length in Chapter 3. Most successful, happy men and women are very good at what they do and they know they are very good. They have learned and practiced and reflected and gotten better and better until they are recognized by their peers as being among the very best in their fields. This feeling of being the best is an absolute prerequisite for deep and lasting self-confidence.

Self-Reliance

The third quality identified in the study was that of self-reliance. Men and women who are respected by others tend to look primarily to themselves for the answers to their questions and for the solutions to their problems. They are highly self-responsible.

They do not blame others or make excuses when things go wrong. They regard themselves as the primary creative forces in their own lives. They volunteer for tough assignments, and they are willing to take charge when something needs to be done.

Intelligence Is More Than IQ

The fourth success quality identified was that of intelligence. Intelligence seems to be a key requirement for success and self-confidence in any field. However, when they looked at this subject, they found that intelligence was not necessarily measured in terms of IQ.

Many of the most notable men and women alive today did poorly in school. They got low grades or no grades, and many of them had not completed university or even high school. One gentleman in the study could not even read or write, and yet he had gotten all the way through university by covering it up and getting others to do his assignments for him.

Income and IQ

In a recent survey in New York, 1,000 adults were selected at random and tested for IQ. It was found that between the person having the highest IQ and the person having the lowest IQ, there was a difference of only two-and-a-half times. But between the person earning the greatest amount of money and the person earning the least amount of money, there was a difference of more than 100 times the income. And the person earning the most was by no means the person with the higher IQ.

How Is Intelligence Defined?

If intelligence is not necessarily IQ, grades, or years of schooling, what is it? In my estimation, intelligence is really a way of acting.

If you act intelligently, you are intelligent. If you act stupidly, you are stupid, regardless of your IQ or your education.

Smart people take the actions necessary to get the results they want. They are effective in whatever situation they find themselves in. Intelligence is more a matter of doing the right things rather than doing things right.

Intelligence Defined

What then is an intelligent way of acting? Here's the answer: An intelligent way of acting is acting in a manner that is consistent with the achievement of your own self-professed goals. Whenever you do something that moves you toward achieving a goal that is important to you, you are behaving intelligently. You are smart.

However, whenever you engage in a behavior that moves you away from one of your own goals, you're behaving stupidly. The world is full of people who are behaving stupidly, hour by hour and day by day, because they are doing things that are guaranteed to bring them the opposite results of what they say they really want.

Make Your Actions Congruent

If one of your goals is to live to be 80 or 90 years old and have a happy, healthy life, then everything that you do today, in terms of your eating, drinking, exercise, rest, and especially avoiding unhealthy behaviors, is smart. However, if you don't exercise, if you eat the wrong foods, smoke cigarettes, and neglect your health in any way, you are behaving stupidly, by your *own* definition.

If you are in sales or business, and you learn how to manage your time well so that you get a lot done in the course of your working day, you are acting intelligently. If you do things that undermine your productivity or move you away from your goals, you are acting foolishly, in terms of your own goals.

Here is a key insight: Everything you do is either moving you toward one of your goals or moving you away from it. Nothing is neutral. *Everything counts.* Each act you engage in is either a positive act that goes on the positive side of your personal balance sheet, or it is a negative act that goes on the negative side of your personal balance sheet.

A great life is simply a life that has far more marks on the positive side than it does on the negative side. This means that an intelligent person is one who does far more things that move him or her toward the things that he or she wants to be, have, and do than an unintelligent person does.

Avoid Self-Delusion

Don't fall into the trap of deluding yourself into believing that only what you want to count counts. Many people think that if they don't count it, it doesn't have any effect on them. They think that if they don't read a book or listen to an audio program, if they don't spend time with their families and play with their children instead of playing on their computers and watching television, if they don't do the things that are leading to a happy, healthy successful life, then somehow, it doesn't matter. It won't count.

The fact is that everything counts. Nothing is neutral. Everything you do or don't do contributes toward making your life a great life or a mediocre life. Everything counts.

With regard to your self-confidence, every time you do something that is moving you in the direction of something that is important to you, you feel a "winner." However, every time you don't do things that move you forward toward something you want or, even worse, moves you away, you feel like a loser.

These behaviors are not only progressive, they are habitual. The more you engage in one behavior or the other, the easier and more automatic that behavior becomes. The more you engage in winning behaviors, the more consistently you act and feel like a winner, the higher will be your self-confidence and the greater will be your belief in yourself and in your goals. Your actions shape your character.

Getting the Job Done

The final quality of success identified in the study was that of result orientation. This means that you know that you are capable of getting the results for which you are responsible. All highly respected men and women are recognized as being the kind of people who can get the job done, whatever it is. They are invariably decisive, results-focused, action-oriented people.

They are performance oriented. They have a bias for action and a sense of urgency. They have trained themselves to be extremely capable at doing whatever is required. Bigger and better jobs and responsibilities seem to flow to them. The world tends to step aside and make way for the person who knows what he or she is doing and knows where he or she is going.

Get Onto the Fast Track

One of the most intelligent things that you can do is to get better at the most important things you do to get the results that determine your success. The better your results, the higher will be your self-confidence and self-esteem. You will be promoted more often and paid more because you will be producing a higher quality and quantity of work.

You will receive more and better job offers. You will be immune to economic downturns because your services will be so valuable. By becoming intensely result oriented, you will guarantee yourself a future of success and prosperity.

Do What the Top People Do

You will notice that everything we have talked about in this book somehow impacts on the five qualities for great success in America. I explained earlier about the importance of selecting your values and organizing your entire life around what you believe to be right and good and true. As long as you know that you are living consistently with your highest principles, your self-confidence rests on an unshakable foundation.

I have talked throughout this book about the importance of setting clear goals and deciding exactly what you want in every area of your life. You know that big, important, challenging goals, clearly defined, with written plans for their accomplishment, improve your overall self-concept and build your self-confidence.

Plan Your Work and Work Your Plan

When you plan your work and work your plan, and dedicate your energies to completing high-value tasks, you start to make rapid progress toward the attainment of your goals; your self-confidence goes up.

Every time you resolve to go the extra mile, to do more than you're paid for, to put in more than you take out, to go beyond what is expected of you in your job and in your relationships with others, you feel terrific about yourself. You feel more like a winner. Your level of self-confidence increases and you feel motivated to contribute even more of yourself to what you are doing.

When you dedicate yourself to becoming better and better at performing the important tasks in your life, you feel an enhanced sense of mastery and competence. Your belief in yourself deepens, and your ability to get the results that are important to you increases. The development of excellence or expertise in what you do is a wonderful form of positive knowing that leads inevitably to higher self-confidence.

Do Your Work Quickly and Well

There is virtually nothing that will bring you the respect and esteem of the people you respect faster than being result oriented and doing your job in an excellent fashion. In study after study, it's been shown that lasting recognition from the important people in your work only comes from being very good at what you do. It is only excellent performance in your job that raises you above politics and gives you the kind of power and influence that really makes a difference in any organization.

Dedicate Yourself to Continuous Learning

Your ongoing commitment to personal and professional development gives you a feeling of continuous growth. Whenever you feel yourself growing as a person, you feel internally motivated and energized to achieve even more. The more you learn, the more you can learn. The more you develop yourself, the more capable you become of further development.

By the law of correspondence, as you become better and more capable on the inside, the outer aspects of your life improve as well. As you see and feel your life getting better, you feel more positive and in control of your own destiny. You like and respect yourself more, and your self-confidence increases.

Take Continuous Forward Action

Any positive, constructive, and self-determined action that you take in the direction of your dreams improves your self-image and raises your self-confidence. When you discipline yourself to do exactly those things that lead you in the direction of what is most important to you, you develop a sense of strength and self-assurance that is evident to the people around you.

Every positive action generates the positive emotion that goes with it. When you keep your thoughts and your actions consistent with your highest aspirations and your most valued goals, you are progressively building the unshakable kind of self-confidence that enables you to accomplish almost anything.

Be Your Own Cheerleader

When you get up each morning, say to yourself, This is going to be a great day! Make the development of a positive personality your over-arching goal and organize all your behaviors in that one direction. Remember, you are demonstrating the highest intelligence when everything you do contributes toward generating the feelings of self-confidence and self-esteem that you desire.

Talk to yourself positively all the time. Say to yourself, "I can do it, I can do it!" Or say, "I feel healthy, I feel happy, I feel terrific!" In your conversations with others, keep your words positive and upbeat. Get away from people who complain and criticize. Make it a game to find something nice to say about everyone and everything. Positive words lead to a positive mental attitude.

Create a positive suggestive environment around yourself. Create clear mental pictures of the person you want to be and the things you want to have. Read books that expand your mind and increase your abilities. Listen to educational audio programs in your car. Get around positive people and get away from negative ones.

Control Your Mental Pictures

Prior to every event of importance, mentally rehearse and see yourself performing at your best in the upcoming situation. Recall and relive a previous excellent performance. Before falling asleep, think about the things you did right during the day and the things you are going to do better in the days to come. Soak your mind in positive images of you at your personal best. What you "see" is what you get.

Whenever something happens that throws you off balance, stabilize yourself by thinking about your goals. Because of the law of substitution, you can only think one thought at a time, and if you think about your goals, your mind will instantly become positive again. Make a game of rising above the petty frustrations of people and traffic and unexpected setbacks. Say to yourself, "What can't be cured must be endured." Get back to thinking about your goals and about what you can do, right now, to move toward them.

Develop Discipline and Courage

Whenever you have the choice of doing what is fun and easy rather than what is hard but necessary, force yourself out of your comfort zone in the direction of your dreams. Consciously resist the temptation to go easy on yourself. Remember that the comfort zone is the great enemy of human performance and human potential. It is only in the areas of challenge and risk that you force yourself just beyond what is comfortable and easy for you, that the possibilities of success await.

Each act of courage and boldness on your part not only builds additional courage and boldness, but it also builds your self-confidence. The more often you dare to go forward, even in the face of uncertainty, the more likely it is that this type of courageous behavior will become a habit for you.

You can gradually act yourself into feeling unafraid in almost all situations. There will very little that that you won't risk or try. You will develop such confidence in yourself that you absolutely believe in your ability to succeed, even against difficult odds. Because success is based on the law of averages, you will ultimately succeed and succeed greatly.

Take Excellent Care of Yourself

Be sure to take good care of yourself physically, every hour and every day. Eat the right foods, drink lots of fluids, get lots of sleep, and exercise regularly. If you're not happy with your physical appearance, go to work to improve it. Set a series of goals to be at your perfect weight, to wear the ideal clothes for you, and to be perfectly groomed in every respect.

Your self-confidence is strongly affected by your self-image. Your self-image, on the other hand, is largely determined by the way you think that other people see you. When you work hard on yourself and take the time to produce an image that you know is attractive to other people, you feel wonderful about yourself and your self-confidence goes straight up. It doesn't matter where you're starting from. Your main job is to decide where it is you want to go and then make a plan to get there.

Speak Up with Confidence and Clarity

In your conversations with others, be sure to speak up clearly, and express yourself openly and honestly. In one-on-one conversations, in meetings, or with groups, the more competent you are at speaking out, the more competent and more confident you will feel.

If shyness is a problem for you, set it as a goal to get over it. Take a Dale Carnegie course on human relationships or join Toastmasters and learn to speak on your feet. Either one, or both, will make you a far more positive, outgoing, and self-confident person.

Practice No-Limit Thinking

You can develop unshakable self-confidence it if you really want to and if you put your mind to it. You can develop within yourself any personality characteristic that you really want. You're always free to choose. Everything you are and everything you become is under your own control.

The final key to self-confidence was put forth by Dorothea Brande in 1935, when she said, "The high road to success is to act as if it were impossible to fail, and it shall be."

The real difference between the winners and losers in life is the difference between taking action and making excuses. It is between the people who do and the people who talk about doing. It is between the movers and shakers and those who just watch the world go by.

Perhaps your greatest responsibility to yourself is to become a person of action—to act yourself into feeling the emotions that are consistent with high-performance.

Your primary job is to make any effort, overcome any obstacle, and scale any height to become the dynamic, unstoppable, irresistibly self-confident person that you are capable of becoming. When you have developed in yourself this unshakable, irresistible quality of self-confidence, everything else will be possible for you.

Action Exercises

1. Resolve today to act as if you had all the self-confidence in the world. Say what you think, ask for what you want, and persist until you succeed.

2. Write down your three most important goals in life right now. Then write down three steps you could take to achieve

each of these goals, and take immediate action on at least one step.

3. Identify the three most important results you achieve in your work, and resolve today to work on those activities most of the time.

4. Create a clear mental picture of yourself performing at your best—calm, confident, and optimistic—and replay this picture over and over throughout the day.

5. Dedicate yourself to continuous personal and professional improvement, getting better every day.

6. Accept 100 percent responsibility for everything you are today, and for everything you become in the future. Refuse to blame anyone for anything.

7. Resolve today that you will never give up, that you will persist over all obstacles until you succeed in creating the wonderful life that is possible for you.

Good luck!

ABOUT THE AUTHOR

Brian Tracy is a professional speaker, trainer, seminar leader, and consultant. He is the chairman of Brian Tracy International, a human resources and development company based in Solana Beach, California.

Brian learned his lessons the hard way. He left high school without graduating and worked as a laborer for several years. In his mid-twenties he became a salesman and began his climb up the business ladder. Year by year, by studying and applying every idea, method, and technique he could find, he worked his way up to become the chief operating officer of a $276-million development company.

In 1981 he began teaching his success principles in talks and seminars around the country. Today, his books, audio programs, and video seminars have been translated into 38 languages and are used in 60 countries.

He is the bestselling author of more than 50 books, including *Create Your Own Future, Change Your Thinking, Change Your Life, Eat That Frog!, Goals, Maximum Achievement, Advanced Selling Strategies, Focal Point,* and *The 100 Absolutely Unbreakable Laws of Business Success.* He has written and produced more than 500 audio and video learning programs that are used worldwide.

Brian is happily married and has four children. He is active in community affairs, and lives in Solana Beach, California.

BRIAN TRACY

Speaker-Author-Consultant

Brian is one of the top professional speakers in the world today. He addresses more than 250,000 people each year throughout the United States, Europe, Asia, and Australia. His keynote speeches, talks, and seminars are described as "inspiring, entertaining, informative, and motivational."

His audiences include businesses and associations of every size and type, including many Fortune 500 companies. Since he began speaking professionally, Brian has shared his ideas with more than five million people in 60 countries, and has served as a consultant and trainer for more than 1,000 corporations. Some of his topics include:

The Psychology of Achievement—How to take control of your life and emotions, become a completely positive, self-confident person, set and achieve all your goals, develop focus and concentration, get along wonderfully with other people, increase your self-esteem, and accomplish more than you ever thought possible.

Twenty-First Century Thinking—How to outthink, out-perform, outsell, and out strategize your competition to get superior results in a turbulent, fast-changing business environment.

Leadership in the New Millennium—How to apply the most powerful leadership principles ever discovered to manage, motivate, inspire, and get better results from and with people, faster than ever before.

Advanced Selling Strategies—How to outthink, outperform, and outsell your competition using the most advanced strategies and tactics known to modern selling.

The Power of Personal Productivity—How to get organized, set clear priorities, focus on key tasks, overcome procrastination, concentrate single-mindedly on your most important tasks, and get more done in a day than many people get done in a week. You learn the strategies and techniques of the most productive people in every field.

For full information on booking Brian to speak at your next meeting or conference, visit Brian Tracy International at www.briantracy.com, or call 858-436-7316 for complete information. Brian will carefully customize his talk for you and for your needs.

INDEX

BUILD A GREAT BUSINESS!

Brian Tracy's Total Business Mastery Seminar

In this two-and-a-half-day Total Business Mastery Seminar—The Two Day MBA, Brian Tracy gives you a practical and immediately actionable, street-smart MBA. You learn the 10 most powerful and important principles for business success, which you can put to work the next day.

Throughout this two-day program, you will work through a series of exercises that enable you to achieve immediate improvements in your sales and profitability. Everything you learn is designed to be applied to your own business, sometimes before the seminar is over.

You'll work on your business and mastermind with your peers to identify your strengths, weaknesses, challenges, and greatest opportunities. You'll leave this seminar with a written plan to increase your sales, reduce your costs, and boost your profits.

You'll learn how to become a more effective executive and generate the critical numbers essential for business success.

You'll learn and internalize the 10 GREAT areas of business success, becoming one of the best businesspeople in your industry.

This entire program can be presented, with all materials, to individuals, corporations, and organizations of almost any size.

For more information go to:
www.briantracy.com/tbm
or call (858) 436-7316

Learn the practical, proven skills and techniques that you need to survive, thrive, and grow in any business and in any market.